"...and distributed it to whoever had need."

(Acts 2:45)

The Biblical Vision of Sabbath Economics

Ched Myers

I am grateful to Kayla McClurg at the Church of the Saviour, Ray McGovern at the Servant Leadership School and Shady Hakim at Bartimaeus Cooperative Ministries for their help in producing this booklet.

For inquiries about the work of Ched Myers and Bartimaeus Cooperative Ministries, contact chedmyers@bcm-net.org or www.bcm-net.org.

First printing
September 2001

Second printing
September 2002

Third printing
September 2004

Fourth printing
September 2006

Fifth printing
September 2007

Sixth printing
December 2008

Seventh printing
January 2012

This booklet is the first in a series of occasional pieces published by *Tell the Word*, a project of the Church of the Saviour. For more information about *Tell the Word* or to be on a subscribers list, contact Kayla McClurg at:

The Church of the Saviour
2025 Massachusetts Avenue NW
Washington, DC 20036
e-mail: office@surfglobal.net
or Bill Banner
Phone: 202-328-0329

Acknowledgements

The chapters of this pamphlet have appeared, in somewhat different forms, as separate articles in the following publications:

Introduction: Excerpted from: "'It is an Issue of Equality...' Biblical Reflections on Wealth and Poverty." Priests and People (England), May, 1999.

Chapter 1: "'God Speed the Year of Jubilee': The Biblical Vision of Sabbath Economics." Sojourners, May-June, 1998.

Chapter 2: "'God Speed the Year of Jubilee': The Biblical Vision of Sabbath Economics." Sojourners, May-June, 1998.

Chapter 3: "Jesus' New Economy of Grace: The Biblical Vision of Sabbath Economics." Sojourners, July-August, 1998.

Chapter 4: "'Who then can be saved?' The Kingdom of God and Redistributive Justice." Christian (Guildford, England), November, 1995.

Chapter 5: Excerpted from: "Towering Trees and 'Talented Slaves'." The Other Side, May-June, 1999. With Eric DeBode.

Chapter 6: Excerpted from: "A Transforming Circle of Story: Recovering Economic Justice in Luke's 'Wilderness Feeding'." Celebration (National Catholic Reporter), June, 2001.

Chapter 7: "Balancing Abundance and Need." The Other Side, Sept-Oct, 1998.

Conclusion: Parts excerpted from "Beyond the 'Addict's Excuse': Public Addiction and Ecclesial Recovery," in The Other Side of Sin, ed. by Susan Nelson and Andrew Sung Park, NY:SUNY Press, 2001.

In memory of Libby Radcliffe
whose life was a gift to us.

---

*[Indigenous people] understood a
cardinal property of the gift:
whatever we have been given is
supposed to be given away again,
not kept…. The essential is this:
the gift must always move…. "One
man's gift," they say, "must not be
another man's capital…."*

Lewis Hyde
*The Gift: Imagination
and the Erotic Life of Property*

Why Sabbath Economics?

"We read the Gospel as if we had no money," laments Jesuit theologian John Haughey, "and we spend our money as if we know nothing of the Gospel." Indeed, the topic of economics is exceedingly difficult to talk about in most First World churches, more taboo than politics or even sex. Yet no aspect of our individual and corporate lives is more determinative of our welfare. And few subjects are more frequently addressed in our scriptures.

The standard of economic and social justice is woven into the warp and weft of the Bible. Pull this strand and the whole fabric unravels. At the heart of this witness is the call to observe what I call "Sabbath economics." At its root, Sabbath observance is about gift and limits: the grace of receiving that which the Creator gives, and the responsibility not to take too much, nor to mistake the gift for a possession. The economic implications of this tradition as it is articulated in the Bible can be summarized in three axioms:

> 1) the world as created by God is abundant, with enough for everyone—provided that human communities restrain their appetites and live within limits;

> 2) disparities in wealth and power are not "natural" but the result of human sin, and must be mitigated within the community of faith through the regular practice of redistribution;

> 3) the prophetic message calls people to the practice of such redistribution, and is thus characterized as "good news" to the poor.

The theology of Sabbath economics and its ethic of regular and systemic wealth and power redistribution—most clearly summed up in the Jubilee release of slaves, deconstruction of debt and return of foreclosed land—is neither utopian nor abstract. It arose out of the concrete Hebrew experience of slavery in Egypt, and so is both *corrective* and *preventative*. I believe it continues to offer communities of faith today a Way out of our historical and persistent slavery to the debt system, with its competing theology of meritocracy and its alienating and cruel practices of wealth and power concentration and social stratification.

Sabbath economics is an unfamiliar notion to First World churches in large part because it has been marginalized by biblical interpreters, whose silence has helped to legitimate the very debt system that the Bible denounces. Skeptical of the Jubilee tradition as irrelevant, unrealistic or threatening, they have not found evidence for its practice in either Testament because they have not been looking for it. This is because, as theologian Wayne Meeks puts it in his excellent book, *God the Economist* (1989), "Our theological imaginations have long been captive to the market-driven orthodoxies of modern capitalism."

> There is a deficit of theological work with regard to political economy. God concepts have been criticized in relation to racism, sexism, the technological mastery of the environment, and ordinary people's loss of the democratic control of their lives. But not enough attention has been given to how God concepts in North Atlantic church and society relate to the deepest assumptions of the market society.

Yet the preeminent challenge to the human family in our time is the increasingly unequal distribution of wealth and power, and any theology that refuses to reckon with these realities is both cruel and irrelevant.

Today the wealthiest 20% of the world's population receives almost 83% of the world's income, while the poorest 20% receive less than 2%! Collins and Veskel (2000), in their concise primer on economic disparity in the U.S. today, tell us that in 1965 the average U.S. worker made $7.52 per hour, while the person running the company made $330.38 per hour. Today, the average worker makes $7.39 per hour, the average CEO $1,566.68 per hour—212 times more! This is "trickle up" economics: the transfer of wealth from the increasingly *poor* to the increasingly *rich*. And neo-liberal policies of "structural adjustment" are not only hardening this income polarization, but also deepening psychic and social alienation. Whether through plant closings, the demise of the local grocery store or the crisis of the family farm, we in the First World are now witnessing the epidemic of communal displacement that has already devastated local culture, institutions and environments in the Third and Fourth Worlds. We Christians *must* talk about economics, and talk about it in light of the gospel.

The good news is that our churches, according to Cornel West, "... may be the last places left in our culture that can engage the public conversation with non-market values." Indeed, the "subversive memory" of Jubilee justice has kept erupting throughout church history. It animated early monks, medieval communitarians and radical Reformers. Even with the ascendancy of modern capitalism—with its fierce antipathy toward Sabbath economics—this vision has not been extinguished. We see it in tracts and tunes by the 18th century "Leveler" Thomas Spence in the struggle against the enclosures (i.e. privatization) of the Commons in early industrial England:

> Since then this Jubilee
> Sets all at Liberty
> Let us be glad
> Behold each man return to his possession!

And we hear it in the 19th century spirituals of African slaves sung in American fields:

> Don't you hear the Gospel trumpet sound Jubilee?

Fortunately today, at the turning of the millennia, the vision of "release from the bondage of debt" is again firing the imaginations of faith-based activists.

Over the last five years efforts to rehabilitate the Jubilee tradition for our time have been growing among those committed to redressing this longstanding and scandalous suppression of "good news" for the poor. This renewal movement is producing new readings of both the Bible and the economy, which are helping to animate popular struggles that range from local living wage campaigns in support of low-income workers to the international Jubilee 2000 Campaign that is educating and organizing in support of debt-relief for impoverished Third World countries. There is a groundswell of alternative consciousness around economics that one can see in the many small-scale experiments here and around the world with more just and environmentally sustainable business practices, technologies, land uses, financial systems, trade patterns, consumption habits, and income distribution schemes. This historical moment, then, offers a unique opportunity for the church to renew its spirituality and its mission to the world.

For the fact is, these are hard times for those trying to resist the triumphant march of a global capitalism that leaves in its wake ever-increasing disparities between rich and poor. It is a struggle to find an alternative language and practice to the manic claims and absolutist grip of market thinking. That means this is a *good* time for the church to rediscover the radically different vision of economic and social practice that lies right at the heart of her scriptures. The Bible recognizes that inequalities will inevitably arise in "fallen" society—a realism it shares with the worldview of modern capitalism. Unlike the social Darwinism of the latter, however, the biblical vision refuses to stipulate that injustice is therefore a *permanent* condition. Instead, God's people are instructed to dismantle, on a regular basis, the fundamental patterns and structures of stratified wealth and power, so that there is enough for everyone.

It was in light of this season of challenge and opportunity for the church that colleagues at the Church of the Saviour in Washington, D.C., and I decided there was a need for a brief and popular survey and summary of the biblical vision of Sabbath economics. This booklet attempts to introduce the variety of ways this tradition is articulated in both testaments: through Exodus storytelling, Levitical legislation, Deuteronomic exhortation, prophetic pronouncement, gospel parable and apostolic pleading. The following material has appeared over the last five years in a variety of Christian publications, and has been assembled and edited here to try to offer a concise overview of Sabbath economics that has both breadth and depth, but that keeps references and technical details to a minimum.

Because of limitations of space, I have not tried to take on here in any detail the crucial question of what practical implications these readings have for our discipleship today. In the Conclusion I do, however, make some brief suggestions about the relevance of the addiction/recovery model to our dilemma, and point toward some resources for further reflection and action. For those wishing fuller treatments of the socio-historical and literary dimensions of the biblical texts surveyed here, I highly recommend the work of biblical scholars (and friends!) Richard Lowery for the Hebrew Bible (*Sabbath and Jubilee*, Chalice Press, 2000), and Sharon Ringe for the gospels (*Jesus, Liberation, and the Biblical Jubilee*, Fortress Press, 1985). For those looking for a more comprehensive and readable treatment of these matters and their relevance for today, I commend Ross and Gloria Kinsler's *The Biblical Jubilee and the Struggle for Life* (Orbis, 1999), which is an excellent resource for study groups.

May this ancient biblical vision indeed animate new possibilities for our history, as invoked in the prayer of the nineteenth century abolitionist, William Lloyd Garrison:

> God speed the year of jubilee, the wide world o'er!
> When from their galling chains set free,
> Th' oppressed shall vilely bend the knee
> And wear the yoke of tyranny, like brutes, no more—
> That year will come, and Freedom's reign
> To all their plundered rights again, restore.

Ched Myers
Pentecost, 2001

9

Chapter One

"What is this?"

Sabbath Economics

in Torah

The standard of social and economic justice in Torah (the first five books of the Hebrew Bible) is grounded in God's call to "keep the Sabbath." The word "Sabbath" comes from the Hebrew verb *shabat,* which means "to rest or stop working." It first appears in the Bible as the culmination of the story of Creation. God creates a world that is "good," but that English adjective is hardly an adequate rendering of the Hebrew term *tov.* It is better translated as "delightful" or "fat" or "incredible"— think of the adjectives you might utter while gazing upon a magnificent sunset or the Grand Tetons or a wild oceanscape. *This* world can be improved upon by no human work—it is abundant, satisfying, magical.

Yet the Creator culminates this "good" work by stopping: "God rested on the seventh day from all the work God did" (Gen 2:2). Hebrew Bible scholar and activist Richard Lowery, in his brilliant *Sabbath and Jubilee* (2000), points out "… in a delightful twist, 'rest' is signified as a verb in this passage and 'work' as a noun." This establishes a primal pattern: good work is followed by Sabbath. It is important to note that this cosmic Sabbath is *not* for the purpose of resting in order to work more;

there is no "Monday" in the Creation narrative. The purpose of this Sabbath is to enjoy the world *forever*, which is why it is "blessed" (2:3), just like the creation itself (1:22,28). Lowery concludes that the Sabbath thus captures the double theme of the creation story: abundance as the divine gift, and self-limitation as the appropriate response.

Human beings are to imitate God in practicing Sabbath. The next place we encounter the term (now as a noun, not a verb) is in the archetypal story of hunger and bread in the wilderness (Ex 16), which is sandwiched between two stories of thirst and water (Ex 15:22-27 and 17:1-7). The Hebrews have been sprung from slavery, but must now face the harsh realities of life outside the imperial system. Their first test of character, not surprisingly, is how they will sustain themselves. The ancient Israelites—like modern North Americans—couldn't imagine an economic system apart from the Egyptian political-military-technological complex that enslaved them. "Would that we had died at the Lord's hand in the land of Egypt, as we sat by our fleshpots and ate our fill of bread! But you have led us into this desert to die of famine" (Ex 16:3).

The manna story is not primarily a feeding miracle, nor a morality tale about trust (as is usually taught in our churches), but a didactic story about the importance of "following instructions" (16:4). It illustrates Yahweh's alternative to the oppressive Egyptian economy (Ex 16:6). "Bread raining from heaven" symbolizes fertility as a Divine gift, a process that begins with rain and ends with bread (see Isaiah 55:10 and the parallel between the wilderness manna and the produce of the settled land in Joshua 5:12). The manna is thus a "test" to see if Israel will follow instructions on how to "gather" this gift. The people's first lesson outside of Egypt, then, is an economic one. I believe it represents a parable about the primal value of the most basic human competence—hunting/gathering and local horticulture—the cooperative, egalitarian lifeway that sustained human beings for tens of thousands of years prior to the rise of concentrated agriculture, cities and eventually imperial economies based on slavery.

The "instructions" in the narrative give us the three defining characteristics of this alternative economic practice. First, every family is told to gather just enough bread for their needs (Ex 16:16-18). In contrast to Israel's Egyptian condition of deprivation, here everyone has *enough*: "Those who gathered more had no surplus, and those who gathered less had no shortage." In God's economy there *is* such a thing as "too much" and "too little." (This contrasts radically with modern capitalism's infinite tolerance for wealth and poverty.) This "theology of enough" is underlined by the (probably later) inverse version of the manna story in Numbers 11, in which the people's lack of limits is punished with a plague of "selfish excess":

> So the people worked all day and night and all
> the next day, gathering the quails; the least
> anyone gathered was ten homers.... But while
> the meat was still between their teeth, before it
> was consumed, the anger of God was kindled
> against the people, and God struck them with a
> very great plague. So that place was called
> *Kibroth-hattaavah*—which means, "the graves
> of craving" (Num 11:32-34; see Psalm 78:20-31;
> 106:13-15).

Second, this bread should not be "stored up" (16:19-20). Wealth and power in Egypt was defined by surplus accumulation. It is no accident that Israel's forced labor consisted of building "store-cities" (Ex 1:11), into which the empire's plunder and the tribute of subject peoples was gathered. (This too prefigures capitalism, whose dictum, according to Marx, was: "Accumulate, accumulate, accumulate—this is the Law and the Prophets!") The Bible understands that dominant civilizations exert centripetal force, drawing labor, resources and wealth into greater and greater concentrations of idolatrous power (an archetypal description of this is found in the story of the Tower of Babel, Gen 11:1-9). So Israel is enjoined to keep wealth *circulating* through strategies of redistribution, not *concentrating* through strategies of accumulation.

The third instruction introduces Sabbath discipline (Ex 16:22-30). "Six days you shall gather; but on the seventh, which is a Sabbath, there will be none" (Ex 16:26). We Christians regard the Sabbath at best as one of the Ten Commandments (Ex 20:8-11), at worst as a quaint Jewish custom. But here we see that it is instituted even *before* the Covenant at Sinai. And at the conclusion of the Covenant Code comes the solemn warning: if the people do not practice Sabbath, they will die (Ex 31:12-17). Not only then is the Sabbath the crowning blessing of creation; it is also the "beginning and end of the Law."

We Christians therefore trivialize (and even "profane") the Sabbath if we regard it merely as a day to do as little as possible, or as an antiquated Jewish code of nit-picking prohibitions. Torah's Sabbath regulations represent God's strategy for teaching Israel about its dependence upon the land as a gift to share equitably, not as a possession to exploit. Thus it is the central rhythm in the public life of the people, as reflected for example in the calendar of festivals (Lev 23). Not only is the weekly Sabbath first among the appointed feasts (Lev 23:3), but community work-stoppages define each of the main observances: Passover (23:6f); *Shavuot* (23:21); Feast of Atonement (23:24,31); and Booths (23:35f).

The prescribed periodic rest for the land and for human labor goes beyond the agricultural good sense of letting land lie fallow. It functions to disrupt human attempts to "control" nature and "maximize" the forces of production. Because the earth belongs to God and its fruits are a gift, the people should justly distribute those fruits, instead of seeking to own and hoard them. "Sabbath observance requires a leap of faith, a firm confidence that the world will continue to operate benevolently for a day without human labor, that God is willing and able to provide enough for the good life," writes Lowery. "Sabbath promises seven days of prosperity for six days of work. It operates on the assumption that human life and prosperity exceed human productivity."

This primal lesson was so fundamental that the people were instructed to keep a jarful of the manna *in front* of the Covenant (Ex 16:32; see Heb 9:4). Sabbath observation means to remember *every week* this economy's two principles: the goal of "enough" for everyone, and the prohibition on accumulation.

The manna story illustrates human dependence upon the divine "economy of grace," not upon human labor, technology or social organization. This vision is, of course, utterly contrary to economics as we know it. Our incredulity is rather humorously anticipated in the story itself: "manna" is a play on words and can be translated, "What *is this?*" (Ex 16:15). But this vision was neither novel nor utopian. The instructions of Exodus 16 could be said to describe the economic culture modern anthropologists call "generalized reciprocity," a subsistence culture of cooperation and sharing that characterized all hunter-gatherer societies from antiquity up to the present.

The social justice code of Exodus 23 extends the Sabbath cycle to a seventh year: "You shall let the land rest and lie fallow, so that the poor of your people may eat; and what they leave the wild animals may eat" (Ex 23:10-11). The Sabbath year restores equilibrium by restraining the activity of "productive" members of the economy and freeing constraints upon those whom the economy has marginalized, both the disenfranchised (the poor) and the undomesticated (wild animals)!

The Deuteronomist goes even further, interpreting the Sabbath year to include debt-release (Dt 15:1-81). This was intended as a hedge against the inevitable tendency of human societies to concentrate power and wealth in the hands of the few, creating hierarchical classes with the poor at the bottom. In agrarian societies such as biblical Israel (or parts of the Third World today), the cycle of poverty began when a family fell into debt, deepened when it had to sell off its land in order to service the debt, and reached its conclusion when landless peasants could only sell their labor, becoming bond-slaves. Since there were no banks in antiquity, it was larger landowners who acted as creditors—and who foreclosed, adding to their holdings. The prophet Isaiah railed against precisely this process of economic stratification by which wealthy creditors "add house to house and field to field, until there is room for no one but you" (Is 5:8). He saw it as a betrayal of Israel's vocation to be "God's pleasant planting; God expected justice, but saw bloodshed" (Is 5:7).

The Sabbath year debt release intends to safeguard both social justice—"there will be no one in need among you"—and

14

sound fiscal policy—"creditor nations will not rule over you" (Dt 15:4-6). But anticipating the human tendency toward selfishness, the practical Deuteronomist specifically forbids people from tightening credit in the years immediately prior to the Sabbath remission (15:7-11). The remission applies to debt-slaves as well, not only freeing them but demanding that they be sent away with sufficient resources to make it on their own (15:12-17). Whether or not the community will enjoy the blessing of the land is contingent on its fidelity to this Sabbath discipline, which Deuteronomy, like Exodus, grounds in the memory of being liberated from Egyptian slavery (Dt 15:15; see 5:15).

The fullest expression of Sabbath logic is the Levitical "Jubilee": a comprehensive remission to take place every "Sabbath's Sabbath" or 49th/50th year (Lev 25). The Jubilee (named after the *jovel*, a ram's horn that sounded to herald the remission) aimed to dismantle structures of social-economic inequality by:

- releasing each community member from debt (Lev 25:35-42);
- returning encumbered or forfeited land to its original owners (25:13,25-28);
- freeing slaves (25:47-55).

The rationale for this unilateral restructuring of the community's assets was to remind Israel that the land belongs to God (25:23) and that they are an exodus people who must never return to a system of slavery (25:42).

The Jubilee was perhaps already prefigured in the "Feast of Weeks" (*Shavuot*, later the feast of Pentecost), a celebration of the first fruits of the harvest (Ex 23:16; Lev 23:15-25; Dt 16:9-12).

> *Feast of Weeks:* From the day after the Sabbath, from the day on which you bring the sheaf of the elevation offering, you shall count off seven weeks.... You shall count until the day after the seventh Sabbath, fifty

days; then you shall present an
offering of new grain to the Lord
(Lev 23:15).

Jubilee: You shall count off seven
weeks of years, seven times seven
years, so that the period ... gives
forty-nine years.... And you shall
hallow the fiftieth year and you
shall proclaim liberty throughout
the land to all its inhabitants (Lev
25:8,10).

This suggests that "Sabbath economics" applied at *each*
harvest, not just every other generation.

Lowery points out that the Sabbath vision is diametrically
opposed to our modern assumptions about economics. The two
main axioms of classical economics are: 1) the natural condition
of scarcity; and 2) unlimited human appetite. These, he writes,
"breed resignation to systems of distribution so unequal as to
guarantee homelessness and starvation. On the other hand, they
create an imperative toward unlimited economic growth."
Sabbath economics, however, based on "... the principles of
abundance and self-restraint turn this classical economic approach on its head. If you assume that resources are abundant,
sufficient for the survival and prosperity of human life, and that
human needs and wants are limited, then no one need starve or
suffer the elements through lack of housing or clothing." The
conclusion we must draw, says Lowery, is that "long-term,
systemic hunger, homelessness and poverty can be viewed only
as a failure of human will."

Our modern economic system is a cruel parody of Sabbath
economics. We have indeed created a situation of "scarcity" in
nature because of our relentless plundering of the land and its
gifts. At the same time, capitalism has demonstrated incredible
ingenuity and capacity to manufacture "artificial abundance"
(think of the 30 kinds of cereal or toothpaste at your local
supermarket). There is enough, but it is no longer a gift of
creation. Rather, it is a marketed commodity, which by definition does not circulate equitably to everyone. Thus we have "re-

engineered" the world: our refusal to limit our appetites has drained natural abundance, and our artificial abundance belongs only to the few. This is not ironic; it is idolatrous.

Kentucky philosopher-farmer Wendell Berry (1990) believes the all-encompassing and integrated system of nature should be understood as "the Great Economy," upon which human systems ("little economies") by necessity depend. The problem, Berry writes, is that our modern industrial economy, with its managerial penchant for control and its lack of limits, "... does not see itself as a little economy; it sees itself as the *only* economy. It makes itself thus exclusive by the simple expedient of valuing only what it can use—that is, only what it can regard as 'raw material' to be transformed mechanically into something else.... The industrial economy is based on invasion and pillage of the Great Economy."

The ecological and social wisdom of Sabbath practice seeks to restore the primacy of the Great Economy, and to force humans to re-adapt to *its* limits. As rabbi Arthur Waskow (1995) puts it, "This *Shabat* betokens the peace agreement ending the primordial war between ourselves and earth which began as we left Eden—which came from a misdeed of eating and brought us painful toil and turmoil in our eating."

Chapter Two

"The spoil of the poor is in your houses!"

The Prophetic Critique

There is an old Bible story about King Josiah of Judah, who is told of "a book of the Law" that has been discovered in the basement of the Temple (II Kings 22). The king summons all his advisors to interpret the meaning of this book. But these luminaries turn immediately for help to an obscure figure: Huldah, the wife of a "keeper of the wardrobe." Mentioned in only this scripture, this woman may be marginal (a seamstress? a hairdresser?), but she is a prophet, and it is *she,* not the royal scribes, who interprets the meaning of the lost book to the king. Her reading represents a hard word of judgment upon the community's apostasy, yet promises renewal if the community's leadership has the courage and vision to face their mistakes and turn their social project back toward the vision of justice. Scholars believe this old story refers to the "appearance" of the book of Deuteronomy, which launched the Josianic reform, a major turning point in the history of Israel.

This story seems a fitting trope for our attempts to rehabilitate the biblical vision of Sabbath economics. It is as if we have stumbled upon an old book that for too long has been gathering dust in our churches. Its words are strange and troubling, and our official interpreters are loath to confront them. We need the wise, strong and discomforting voice of the marginalized to help the old tradition make sense to us—and then we must act differently.

So it is with the Sabbath/Jubilee tradition in First World Christianity. Skeptical of any voice that is critical of our Capitalist Paradise, we have not seen the footprints of Jubilee practice throughout the Bible because we were not looking for them (rather we were looking for affirmation of our affluence). Indeed, in the North American church our fears have persuaded us that the biblical Jubilee is at best utopian, and at worst Communistic. Yet we find it awkward simply to dismiss the biblical witness, so an alternative objection inevitably arises: "Israel never really *practiced* the Jubilee!" If genuine, and not simply a strategy of avoidance, this challenge is best addressed by considering both the "negative" and "positive" evidence.

The primary "negative" evidence is the manner in which Israel's prophets repeatedly and relentlessly criticized the nation's leadership for betraying the poor and the vulnerable members of the community. This public criticism strongly suggests that the Sabbath vision of social and economic justice remained a measuring stick to which they could appeal.

There can be no question that the Sabbath disciplines of seventh year debt release and Jubilee restructuring were regularly abandoned by those Israelites who wished to consolidate social advantages they had gained. The historical narratives in the Hebrew Bible indicate that as the tribal confederacy was eclipsed by centralized political power under the Davidic dynasty, economic stratification followed inexorably. Indeed, the prophet Samuel warned that a monarchy would be linked intrinsically to an economy geared to the elite through ruthless policies of surplus-extraction and militarism (I Sam 8:11-17a). If, Samuel lamented, Israel insisted on recreating this "Egyptian condition" among themselves, their Liberator God would no longer hear their cries (I Sam 8:17b-18).

Israel's abandonment of its Sabbath vocation became a central complaint of the prophets. When Isaiah charged the nation's leadership with robbery—"The spoil of the poor is in your houses; what do you mean by crushing my people, by grinding the face of the poor?" (Is 3:14f)—he was echoing the manna tradition's censure of stored wealth in the face of community need (see also Mal 3:5-12). In his most famous parable, Isaiah uses the metaphor of a mismanaged vineyard to savagely attack the ruling classes for the way in which they have used the mechanisms of debt and foreclosure to "latifundialize" the political economy of land (that is, consolidate their holdings while the poor become landless): "Woe to you who join house to house and field to field until no space is left and you live alone in the land" (Is 5:8). This bitter denunciation makes little sense if the Sabbath strictures on accumulation were not part of the people's consciousness. Jesus of Nazareth will, centuries later, rehabilitate and recontextualize Isaiah's parable in his own warning to the Jerusalem elite (Mk 12:1ff).

Amos accused the commercial classes of regarding *shabat* as an obstacle to market profiteering instead of keeping the Sabbath holy: "We will make the *ephah* small and the *shekel* great, and practice deceit with false balances" (Amos 8:5f). The rich and landed treat the poor as an exploitable class instead of guaranteeing their gleaning rights (see Ex 23:10f; Lev 19:9; Mic 7:1), "buying the poor for silver and the needy for a pair of sandals, and selling sweepings of the wheat" (Amos 8:6).

Hosea laments that fidelity to international markets had replaced Israel's allegiance to God's economy of grace: "I will go after my lovers; *they* give me my bread and my water, my wool and my flax, my oil and my drink" (Hosea 2:5). Most telling of all, however, is the tradition that attributed the downfall of Jerusalem to the people's failure to keep Sabbath: "God took into exile in Babylon those who had escaped the sword ... to fulfill the word of the Lord by the mouth of Jeremiah, until the land *had made up for its Sabbaths*. All the days that it lay desolate it kept Sabbath, to fulfill seventy years" (II Chron 36:20f; see Lev 26:34f).

But there is also positive evidence that the Sabbath vision was practiced. Jeremiah blasts King Zedekiah when he reneges on his declaration of Jubilee manumission:

Thus says the Lord: "I myself made a covenant
with your ancestors when I brought them out of
the land of Egypt ... saying, 'Every seventh year
each of you must set free any Hebrews....' But
your ancestors did not listen to me.... You
yourselves recently repented and did what was
right in my sight by proclaiming liberty to one
another ... but then you turned around and
profaned my name when each of you took back
your slaves" (Jer 34:13-16).

Naboth resists King Ahab's attempt to assert eminent
domain by invoking his traditional "ancestral rights" to the land
(I Kg 21). And the reformer Nehemiah resurrects the Levitical
prohibition of interest (Neh 5:6-13) as well as the Sabbath
strictures on commercial production, transaction and finance:
"...if the peoples of the land bring in merchandise or any grain
on the Sabbath day to sell, we will not buy it ... and we will
forego the crops on the seventh year and the exaction of every
debt" (Neh 10:31). Even in late second Temple Judaism we find
allusion to the Sabbath Year in the Book of Jubilees and in the
writings of the Jewish historian Josephus.

The Sabbath also functioned symbolically in the legends of
Israel. The number seven is of course archetypal throughout the
Hebrew Bible, prominent for example in the stories of Noah
(Gen 7-8), Samson (Jud 14,16), Elijah (I Kg 18:43f), Elisha (II
Kg 4:35; 5:10-14), and Esther (Est 1-2). Most famous is the
story of Joshua's assault of the formidable Canaanite fortress of
Jericho. God instructs the Hebrew rebels to march around the
city for seven days, and on the seventh day they march around it
seven times while trumpeting the *jovel*, after which the walls
famously come a-tumblin' down (Josh 6). Not only is this story
a hilarious parody of ancient military tactics of siege-laying, the
Jubilee symbolism could not be clearer. The fortress city represents Canaanite political and economic hegemony over the
hinterlands; the Jubilee circle dance of Joshua represents the
alternative vision of liberation from the oppressive system of
exacted agricultural tribute.

Finally, there are eschatological visions of Jubilee. Sabbath redistribution is remembered by Ezekiel: "My princes shall no longer oppress my people, but shall let the house of Israel have the land according to their tribes" (Ez 45:8; see 46:17f; 47:13ff). The most well-known appropriation of the Jubilee vision is found in Isaiah 61:1-2: the prophetic commission that begins with a call to "bring good news to the oppressed poor" and ends with a proclamation of "the year of the Lord's favor." Of all the possibilities in his scriptures, it is *this* text that Jesus of Nazareth chose to define and inaugurate his mission, according to Luke's gospel (Lk 4:18-19). And it is in this latter-day Hebrew prophet that the vision of Sabbath economics is wholly rehabilitated, as we shall see in the following chapters.

It is important to point out that many of the Hebrew Bible texts I have cited probably did not take their final form until after the Babylonian Exile (6th century, BCE). This means that the ancient vision of Sabbath economics that originated among tribal Israel was *re-visioned* almost half a millennium later, under very different circumstances. It is a radical vision that has continued to surface among justice-seeking Jews and Christians ever since.

Once we restore Sabbath economics to its central place in the Torah, we hear its echoes *everywhere* in the rest of scripture. If we are going to dismiss the Jubilee because Israel practiced it only inconsistently, we should also ignore the Sermon on the Mount because Christians have rarely embodied Jesus' instruction to love our enemies. But it is time to move beyond such rationalizing theology in our churches. We must rediscover the gospel as good news for the poor, and the economic disciplines of *shabat* as the path of humanization.

Chapter Three

"The Sabbath was created for humanity..."

Jesus and Sabbath Economics

It was the late Mennonite theologian John Howard Yoder, in his now-classic work *The Politics of Jesus* (1972), who popularized for our generation the notion of Jesus as a Jubilee practitioner. Yoder rightly pointed out that Luke's gospel is organized around the Isaiah 61 proclamation of "good news *for the poor*" (Lk 4:16-21). Only real debt-cancellation and land-restoration could represent *good* news to poor people (see Lk 7:22; 14:13,21). Similarly, a Jubilee gospel is usually unwelcome news to the wealthy—as in the Magnificat's annunciation that God "... has filled the hungry with good things, and sent the rich away empty" (Lk 1:53; see Mk 10:22). No doubt it is our discomfort that has led us to relentlessly spiritualize the plain meaning of these texts—against the specific advice of James 2:15f.

Much has been written about the so-called "Nazareth manifesto" in Luke 4 (see Prior, 1995), but the evidence for Jesus' re-visioning of Sabbath economics goes far beyond this and a few other widely acknowledged texts, such as the call to debt-release at the heart of the Lord's Prayer (Mt 6:11f). Jubilee consciousness defined Jesus' call to discipleship, lay at the heart of his teaching, and stood at the center of his conflict with the Judean public order.

The gospels agree that Jesus' first substantive clash with the authorities arose as a result of his practice of "unlicensed" forgiveness of sins, which has clear Jubilee overtones (Mk 2:1-12; Jn 5:9-17). Although the words "sin" (*hamartia*) and "debt" (*opheileema*) are different in Greek, they are the same word in Aramaic, the language of Jesus. Thus we can see many indications of their semantic and social equivalence in the gospels, as for example in the Lord's Prayer according to Luke: "Forgive us our *sins,* for we ourselves forgive everyone *indebted* to us" (Lk 11:4). Their correlation is further suggested by the fact that here and throughout the NT the same verb (*aphiemi*) is used to "forgive" sin and "release" from debt.

Unlike our society, in which the economic dimensions of moral and criminal dysfunction are widely ignored, the gospels do *not* spiritualize "sin" and ignore the realities of "debt," but rather see the two as fundamentally interrelated. We see this in Luke's version of the story of the "woman of the street" who washes Jesus' feet with her hair (Lk 7:36-50). Jesus prefaces his "absolution" of the woman's sins (vv 39,48f) with a Jubilee-type story describing how a creditor forgave debt (vv 41-43). Apparently Jesus was cognizant of the fact that it is usually economic marginalization that drives persons into survival strategies such as prostitution—unlike his male colleagues at the dinner party, who refuse to "see" the circumstances of the woman (7:44). Jesus' shocking commendation of her care, in sharp contrast to his criticism of his male host's failure to observe the basic traditions of hospitality further underline this story as an object lesson in Jubilary social leveling (7:44-46).

Matthew's instructions on reconciliation within the community of faith exhort disciples to forgive sins "seventy times seven," an allusion to the Jubilary "seven times seven" of Lev 25:8 (but also to the primal spiral of vengeance recorded in Gen 4:24). This teaching is then illumined by a thoroughly political-economic tale about the settling of accounts in the debt system (Mt 18:15-35). In this cautionary tale Jesus warns his followers not to think that individual acts of debt-forgiveness alone have the power—no matter how noble or how far up the hierarchy—to transform deeply embedded social systems of indebtedness. This story alludes to royal practices of debt-amnesty that were not uncommon in antiquity as a form of social control and conflict management—but which left the system of economic stratification intact.

In Mark's gospel Jesus identifies himself as the "Human One" who has the authority to forgive sins/debts (Mk 2:10). Shortly thereafter Jesus instructs his disciples to help themselves to field produce, justifying it on the basis of a story about the right of hungry Israelites to food regardless of social convention (Mk 2:23-26). Then comes his punch line: "The Sabbath was created for humanity" (2:27). This is neither a proprietary statement nor a Messianic abrogation of the Sabbath discipline. Quite the contrary: It reiterates the Sabbath as part of the order of God's good creation (Gen 2:2f), and confirms that its purpose is to *humanize us* in a world where so much of our socio-economic reasoning and practice is dehumanizing. Jesus then asserts his authority to interpret true Sabbath practice (Mk 2:28). In fact, Jesus' central struggle with the political leadership was not over theology, but over the meaning of Sabbath (Mk 3:1-6; Lk 13:10-17; Jn 7:22f; 9:14-16). This "Human One," claiming the authority to cancel debts and to restore the Sabbath, is a Jubilee figure indeed!

Jesus' Jubilee orientation is also seen in his efforts to rebuild community between socio-economically alienated groups. His "outreach" to tax collectors, who made their living exploiting debtors, is a case in point. Luke begins and ends his narrative of Jesus' ministry with such stories. Following Jesus' call to discipleship, Levi renounces his tax-collecting work and throws a banquet for Jesus and his clientele of "sinners" (5:27-32). Why does this provoke strenuous protests from the authorities? The answer is made explicit in the story of Zacchaeus (Lk 19:1-10). This wealthy creditor is also invited to host Jesus, but he (rightly) understands this to mean he must first practice substantial economic reparation. It is to this program of socio-economic "leveling" that the official adjudicators of debt object—in Jesus' day and in our own.

But while Levi and Zacchaeus embrace Jubilee liberation through redistribution, another man with "much property" rejects it (Mk 10:21-23), a story so notorious in Christendom that it will be treated on its own (see Chapter Four). Jesus expects his followers to enter into the new economy of grace. Interestingly, the formulaic discipleship phrase "they *left* and followed" (Mk 1:18-20; Lk 5:28) uses the verb *aphiemi,* which we have seen also means to forgive sin/cancel debt. Jesus promises that whoever *leaves* "house or family or fields" (the symbols of the basic agrarian economy: site of consumption, labor force, site of production) will receive the same back "hundredfold" (Mk 10:29f).

Discipleship thus means forsaking the seductions and false securities of the Debt system for a re-communitized economy of generalized reciprocity of sharing and cooperation. This ethos survived then (and still today) only among kindred relations—indeed our word "economics" comes from the Greek term *oikonomia,* or "law of the household." This is why Jesus seeks to form in his community an identity of fictive kinship (Mk 3:31-34): to call each other brother and sister obligates us to *treat* each other according to the economic ethos of the *oikos.* In such an economy, which Jesus identifies with the "Kingdom," there are no longer any rich and poor—by definition, therefore, the rich "cannot enter" it (Mk 10:23-25). So contrary is this vision to our accepted horizons of possibility, however, that disciples ancient and modern have difficulty truly believing (10:26f). Jesus' call for radical social restructuring at all levels, from the household to the body politic (Mk 10:35-45), is summarized by the Jubilee ultimatum: "Many who are first will be last, and the last first" (Mk 10:31).

He typically chooses the venue of table fellowship in order to both show and tell object lessons that illustrate this. Meals lay at the heart of ancient society: where, what and with whom you ate defined your social identity and status. Thus the table was a "mirror" of society, with its economic classes and political divisions. In the extended banquet story in Luke 14 Jesus systematically undermines prevailing conventions and proprieties, while advocating a new "table" of compassion and equality. The opening episode deals (not surprisingly) with a dispute over Sabbath practice (Lk 14:1-6). Next comes Jesus' attack on the dominant system of meritocracy, with its hierarchies, prestige posturing and ladder-climbing, and his invitation to "downward mobility" (vv 7-11). He then offends his host by criticizing his guest list, rejecting the reciprocal patronage system of the elite and calling instead for a focus upon "those who cannot repay" (vv 12-14). The series concludes with Jesus' pointed little fable about an exemplary host who finally understands the bankruptcy of meritocracy, and decides instead to build a Jubilee community with the poor and outcast (vv 15-24).

There is no theme more common to Jesus' storytelling than Sabbath economics. He promises poor sharecroppers abundance (Mk 4:3-8,26-32), but threatens absentee landowners (Mk 12:1-12) and rich householders (Lk 16:19-31) with judgment. In order to emphasize the incompatibility of the economy of grace with the dictates of "Mammon," Jesus spins a parable that portrays a hapless middleman caught in the brutal logic of the debt system who decides to "trade" instead in Jubilee-style debt-release (Lk 16:1-13). When faced with a dispute over inheritance rights, Jesus counters with a parable about the folly of storing up wealth (remember the manna!), and then exhorts us to learn the lessons of grace and subsistence from the "great economy" of nature (Lk 12:13-34; see James 5:1-6). And the infamous parable of the talents/pounds (Mt 25:14-30/Lk 19:11-28) shows how Sabbath perspective as an interpretive key can rescue us from a long tradition of both bad theology and bad economics. This story is again so notorious in capitalist religion that it will be treated separately (see Chapter Five).

In light of this evidence, it should come as no surprise that the archetypal manna story, which as we saw earlier represents the foundation for Sabbath economics, should have a central place in Jesus' consciousness. At the outset of his ministry Jesus must face again the wilderness temptation concerning bread and sustenance (Mt 4:1-4 = Dt 8:2-3 = Ex 16). At the heart of the prayer he teaches his disciples is the double petition: "Give us enough bread for today, and forgive us our debts as we forgive others" (Mt 6:11-12). And at key junctures he re-enacts the old wilderness feeding—and all who participate "have enough" (Mk 6:42; 8:8). This tradition, and its connections to both Hebrew Bible antecedents and the gospel Last Supper, will be examined in Chapter Six.

Finally, no overview of the gospels can be complete without some mention of the most oft-uttered objection to economic justice heard in our churches, namely Jesus' alleged resignation to the fact that "the poor will always be with you" (Mk 14:7). Preachers and politicians alike have used this text to justify disparities in wealth, as if Jesus is stipulating that poverty is predetermined as a condition of nature or, worse, as part of the divine plan. This is a classic case of wrenching a text out of context for purposes of pretext!

The notorious phrase appears in Mark's version of the woman who anoints, a scene which (we would do well to note) takes place among the poor—at the house of a leper (14:3). It occurs as Jesus' disciples scold him for allowing gratuitous waste, namely enjoying expensive ointment that could "be sold and given to the poor" (14:5). Though apparently they have grasped his concern for economic justice, the disciples have yet again failed to understand his practice of radical inclusion, not to mention his commitment to the Way of the Cross! The inflection of Jesus' famous response is key: "The poor will always be *with you*, and whenever *you* want, you can do the right thing by them." This is a statement about the social location of the church, not about the inevitability of poverty!

This is confirmed by the fact that Jesus is here alluding to the Deuteronomic tradition of Sabbath year debt-release (Dt 15:1-8; see Chapter One). The vision of that legislation was that if Sabbath economics were practiced by the community, "there will be no one in need among you" (Dt 15:4). But the practical Deuteronomist, anticipating rightly that the people would forever be hedging on the demands of social justice, sounds a tone of realism by reminding us that compassion is the plumbline of this legislation: "But because there will never cease to be needy ones in your land, I command you: open your hand to the poor" (Dt 15:11). The same dialectical reasoning defines Sabbath economics throughout the Bible: the divine vision is that poverty be abolished, but as long as it persists, God and God's people must always take the side of the poor.

These are just some of the "Jubilee footprints" in the Jesus story. Let us now turn to take a closer look at three gospel moments—a call to discipleship in Mark, a parabolic teaching from Matthew, and an example of Jesus' symbolic action in Luke—in order to examine the relationship between Jesus and Sabbath economics more carefully.

Chapter Four

"You lack only one thing."

The Call of the Rich Man and The Kingdom of God in Mark

The story of Jesus and the rich man (Mk 10:17-31) lies at the crossroads of Mark's gospel narrative. From there Jesus will turn toward Jerusalem, a destination of confrontation with the Powers that evoked dread and denial among Jesus' disciples then (10:32) as now. But the encounter between Jesus and this affluent gentleman represents a theological crossroad as well.

The man's question—"What must I do to inherit eternal life?"—is a straightforward inquiry about salvation (10:17). But Jesus neither opens his arms in universal enfranchisement, as in the tradition of modern liberal theology, nor does he demand proper belief, as conservative theology dictates. Instead, Jesus challenges him, equally straightforwardly, to redistribute his assets to the poor. An encounter that began with such theological promise thus concludes with the man's decisive *rejection* of discipleship (10:22). Worse, Jesus seems to shrug it off with a crude class explanation: "How difficult it is for the wealthy to enter the Kingdom of God" (10:24).

This story is all too familiar to Christendom, yet has never seemed to be overly troubling. Perhaps this is because theologians have spent so much intellectual energy undermining its plain meaning. The text has occasioned countless homilies on how those who are blessed with wealth must take care not to let their affluence get in the way of their love for God and the church—despite the fact that such an interpretation is *precisely* what this text rejects out of hand. How might we rescue this story from such domestication? We might begin by changing our focus, as does the text itself, from the rich man's concern about eternal life to Jesus' concern about the "Kingdom of God." Now, however, we have another problem, because how we should understand the gospel notion of the Kingdom of God has been no small debate among New Testament scholars. Indeed, for most North American theologians the Kingdom has represented little more than a nebulous, eschatological metaphor that can be attached to any variety of idealism as easily as ignored altogether.

Mark's use of Kingdom language is relatively sparing and somewhat slippery. Sometimes it is portrayed in *temporal* terms: it is an imminent *kairos* (1:15), a powerful moment of revelation (9:1), a future "blessed hope" (14:25). Other times Mark suggests the Kingdom is more *spatial* in character: a place into which one *enters* (9:47; 10:23f) and/or a "state of being" which one *receives* (10:14f). It is *paradoxical*: for disciples it is a "mystery," and for others it is a "parable" (4:11). Yet the Kingdom of God is nevertheless *concrete*. When pressed for an analogy, Mark's Jesus chooses not some arcane symbol but the reality most familiar to poor folk: the land itself (4:26,30).

We are, in short, never really told definitively what the Kingdom of God *is* by Mark. He does, however, at one point make it clear what it is *not*. So the audience will not forget— repetition being the key to pedagogy—Jesus offers a lyrical little verse, whose point is sharpened with the razor's edge of absurdist humor:

> How <u>difficult</u> it will be for those with <u>riches</u>
> *to enter the Kingdom of God!*
> . . . Children, how <u>difficult</u> it is
> *to enter the Kingdom of God!*
> It is easier for a camel to go through a needle's eye
> than for a <u>rich man</u>
> *to enter the Kingdom of God!* (10:23-25)

Whatever else the Kingdom of God may be, it is plainly where the rich are *not*! Today we North American Christians, who can only be defined as rich relative to the global distribution of wealth and power, would do well to reflect at length on this terrifying triplet. For it remains as dissonant to our ears today as it was to the disciples in the story, provoking the same kind of astonishment (10:23,26).

The clarity of this text has somehow escaped the church through the ages, which instead has concocted a hundred ingenuous reasons why it cannot mean what it says. Christians have been so anxious that Jesus might be saying something exclusive or critical about the rich that they have missed the fact that this triplet is not a statement about *them* at all. It is a statement about the nature of the *Kingdom*. These reiterations—all in the indicative mood—insist that the Kingdom of God is simply that social condition *in which there are no rich and poor*. By definition, then, the rich cannot enter—not, that is, with their wealth intact.

To understand this, let us take a closer look at the whole episode. From his direct approach to Jesus we can tell that the man is socially powerful; he wants something and is willing to give deference in exchange (10:17). But his grandiose claim to innocence ("I have kept all the commandments," 10:20) flies in the face of Jesus' own rejection of his original compliment ("No one is good but God alone," 10:18). Moreover, the religious concern reflected in his original inquiry is not as genuine as it appeared at first glance. The problem is that his question assumes he can *inherit* eternal life. The root of this verb (Greek, *kleeronomeoo*) is *kleeros*, a parcel of land. In some Hellenistic literature this term is synonymous with *kteema*, "real property," which appears in Mk 10:22. This gentleman, in other words, appears to be exhibiting characteristics associated with the "false consciousness" of class entitlement. For him, eternal life, like property, must be *inherited*.

Beneficiaries of a socio-economic system often envision religion as a reproduction of their own privilege (hence Marx's contention that "material life determines consciousness"). In the case of this man, we are told "he possessed many

32

properties" (10:22). Indeed in first century Palestine, land (not commodities) was the basis of wealth. The tiny landed class of Jewish Palestine took great care to protect its entitlement from generation to generation. As Jesus later suggests in a parable about the struggle over deeded land, in which insurgent tenants try to kill the *kleeronomos* in order to wrest the *kleeronomis* from the absentee landlord, the politics of inheritance was often a bloody business (Mk 12:7).

This story is more interested in *how* this man became so affluent than in his pious claims. The estates of the rich grew in several ways. Assets were sometimes consolidated through the joining of households in marital or political alliances. Other times expropriated land was distributed through political patronage. But as noted in Chapter One, the primary mechanism was acquiring land through the debt-default of the poor. Small agricultural landholders groaned under the burden of rent, tithes, taxes, tariffs and operating expenses. If they fell behind in payments, they were forced to take out loans secured by their land. When unable to service these loans, the land was lost to the lenders. These lenders were in most cases the large landowners, who in the absence of banking institutions made available their surplus capital. This is how socio-economic inequality had become so widespread in the time of Jesus (criticized in Mk 4:24f). It is almost certainly how this man ended up with "many properties." Mark has given us a concise portrait of this man's ideology of *entitlement*.

This brings us to another overlooked piece of the story: Jesus' "short list" of the Decalogue (10:21). That he leaves out the first four "theological" commandments is unremarkable, since their meaning was not a matter of debate for Jews. The twist lies in the last of the six "ethical" commands—"do not covet what belongs to your neighbor" (Ex 20:17). In Jesus' recitation it has been replaced by an allusion to the Levitical censure, "Do not defraud" (Mk 10:19). This commandment appears in a section of Torah that concerns socio-economic conduct in the Sabbath community:

> You shall not defraud your neighbor; you shall
> not steal; you shall not keep for yourself the
> wages of a laborer (Lev 19:13).

With this deft bit of editorial interpretation, Mark's Jesus suddenly snaps into focus the cycle of indebtedness just described. The implication is that the "propertied" create and maintain their surplus through "fraud." They may justify their wealth by ideologies of entitlement, but Jesus unmasks it as the result of illegitimate expropriation of their neighbor's land.

"Jesus looked at the man and loved him" (10:21). Now comes the hard truth that arises from Jesus' genuine compassion, the kind of love that refuses to equivocate. "You *lack* one thing." The word here (Greek, *husterei*) implies that it is this man who is in debt—to the poor he has defrauded. The rich man, in the logic of the Kingdom, is poor (see for example the destitute poverty, *hustereeseoos*, of the widow in 12:44, there also contrasted with the wealthy). "Get up," pleads Jesus—this is the verb Mark uses most often for healing episodes. "Sell what you have, give to the poor, and come follow me." That is, he must de-construct the fraudulent system from which he derives his privilege and restore to the poor what has been taken from them. By redistributing his ill-gotten surplus, he stands to receive "*treasure* in heaven" (Greek, *theesauron*, a term distinct from the other three words used to describe wealth in this episode). We might say that Jesus has just radically revalued the currency!

Jesus is not inviting this man to change his attitude toward his wealth, nor to treat his servants better, nor to reform his personal life. He is asserting the precondition for discipleship: economic justice. Stung, the man whirls and slinks away (10:22). In the epilogue to the story Jesus turns and looks at the disciples, perhaps bemused at their incredulity. He then offers his little ditty about the Kingdom of God, summarily dismissing the worldview that equates wealth and power with divine blessing or human meritocracy.

It is little wonder the disciples can only muster an anguished protest (10:26). Here we have arrived at the reason why the discourse of the Kingdom of God has circulated at such a low rate of exchange within modern Christianity. In capitalism, redistributive justice is high heresy—but Mark's Jesus has clearly equated it with the Kingdom of God. Those who are structurally advantaged within a given socio-economic system, therefore, by definition cannot be a part of it. Conversely, to practice redistributive justice is not to be saved by works but to celebrate the new "economy of grace."

I would contend that Jubilee ideology is the only plausible background to the practice of Jesus. From the outset of Mark's narrative, Jesus is portrayed as practicing and exhorting Jubilee redistribution. For example, the narrative sequence of Mk 2:1-3:6 is an extended exposition concerning Sabbath economics in the discipleship community. It begins with Jesus' unilateral disposition of sin/debt (2:5). When the scribes, who control the debt system, warn Jesus that "only God can forgive sin," they are placing redistributive justice beyond the pale of history while protecting their own adjudicatory privileges (2:7). In contrast, Jesus asserts that "the Human One has authority on earth" to deconstruct the condition of indebtedness (2:10).

The next episode portrays *debt-collectors* at table with the *indebted* (2:13-17). This is strange fellowship indeed—*unless* Levi was practicing Jubilee as the precondition to his discipleship. This leads to an action in which the disciples commandeer food from a grainfield (2:23ff). There Jesus again asserts the Human One's authority—specifically in relation to Sabbath economics as the practice of surplus redistribution (2:27). The sequence culminates in Jesus' Deuteronomic ultimatum to the synagogue leadership (3:4, see Dt 30:15ff).

Sabbath economics receives still more articulation in the parable of the sower (the "hundredfold" harvest in 4:8 represents abundance) and the manna-action in the wilderness ("everyone had enough," 6:42). Indebted peasants are liberated and the hungry are fed when we break free of the determinations of the market (6:36f). These themes appear again later in Mark's story in Jesus' criticism of the way in which the central institution of the Judean political economy, the Jerusalem Temple, exploits the poor instead of redistributing the community's wealth (see 11:11-25; 12:38-13:2).

The "inverse economics" (the "last are first") of the Jubilee have been well established in Mark's narrative, then, by the time Jesus invites the rich man to relinquish control over his surplus. He does not "follow," but the disciples remind Jesus that *they have* "left everything and followed" (10:28). Indeed, the word used back in 1:18,20 when the fishermen "left" their nets (Greek *aphienai*) also means "to release" from sin/debt (as in 2:5,7,9). This further knits together the theme of discipleship and economic justice in Mark.

In conclusion to the rich man story, Mark shows that the "hundredfold" harvest promised in the sower parable (4:8) was not a pipedream offered to poor peasants, but the concrete result of wealth redistribution. This surplus is created when the entitlements of *household* (basic productive economic unit), *family* (patrimony and inheritance) and *land* (the basic unit of wealth) are "left"—that is, restructured as community assets (10:29f). "Whosoever" practices this Jubilee/Kingdom way will *receive* (not inherit) the community's abundant sufficiency—an allusion to the divine economy of grace. A note of realism is included: persecution will be the inevitable result of such subversive practice. The matter of eternal life, however, is left for "the age to come" (10:30).

This is the answer to the rich man's question. But he has not stuck around to hear it. He has chosen to retain control over his property, unpersuaded by this alternative vision and thus unwilling to change his economic practice. This illustrates another point of Jesus' sower parable: People *of that class* "hear the word, but the anxieties of this age, the love of riches, and the lust for everything else choke the word, so that it proves unfruitful" (4:19). In Mark, the privileged can enter the Kingdom of God neither through "intellectual assent" (as with the scribe in 12:34) nor "openness" (as with Josephus in 15:43), and they certainly cannot *inherit* it. Reparation—the concrete practice of restoring to the poor what is theirs by rights of community justice—is their only way "in." The moral to the rich man story simply reiterates the essence of Jubilee: "The last will be first" (10:31).

Privately controlled wealth is the backbone of capitalism, and it is predicated upon the exploitation of natural resources and human labor. Profit maximization renders socio-economic stratification, objectification and alienation inevitable. According to the gospel, however, those who are privileged within *this* system cannot enter the Kingdom. This is *not* good news for First World Christians—because we are the "inheritors" of the rich man's legacy. So the unequivocal gospel invitation to repentance is addressed to us. To deconstruct our "inheritance" and redistribute the wealth as reparation to the poor—*that* is what it means for *us* to follow Jesus.

"Who, then, can be saved?" (Mk 10:26). The disciples' incredulity at Jesus' teaching anticipates our own. Does Jesus *really* expect the "haves" (that is, us) to participate in Sabbath wealth redistribution as a condition for discipleship? Can we imagine a world in which there are no rich and poor? To the disciples' skepticism, and to ours, Jesus replies simply: "I know it seems impossible to you, but for God all things are possible" (10:27). In other words, economics is ultimately a theological issue.

Chapter Five

"Talented" Slaves

Bringing a Notorious Parable Back Down to Earth

*Let the wise also hear and gain
in learning, and the discerning
acquire skill to understand
mashal and figure, the words of
the wise and their riddles.*
Prov 1:5-6

The parables of Jesus as preserved in the synoptic gospels represent the very oldest traditions in the New Testament. Despite this (or perhaps because of it), our churches still handle these stories timidly, and often not at all. Perhaps we intuit that there is something so wild and subversive about these tales that they are better kept safely at the margins of our consciousness.

Large numbers of Christians simply ignore the parables, believing that Jesus' teaching was eclipsed by later theological developments: either by his work on the Cross (evangelicals), or by Pauline doctrine as read through the Enlightenment (mainstream Protestants), or by the Church and its Magisterium, (Catholics). The parables are thus apprehended as quaint, or poetic, or theologically figurative—but hardly relevant or substantive for Christian discipleship. Most

38

churches that do attend to gospel parables spiritualize them tirelessly, typically preaching them as "earthly stories with heavenly meanings." Stories about landless peasants and rich landowners, or lords and slaves, or lepers and lawyers are thus lifted out of their social and historical context and reshaped into theological or moralistic fables bereft of any political or economic edge—or consequence.

When the socio-cultural context of the parable is ignored or suppressed, however, we inevitably recontextualize the story in terms of our own unconscious political assumptions. While our imposed schemas often defy the coherence of the text itself, this interpretive strategy functions to thoroughly domesticate the parable under *our* status quo. Stories meant to challenge our preconceptions are thus used to legitimate them. So do we disarm the gospel's most powerful rhetorical weapons, whose purpose is to rescue believers from *our* domestication by that same status quo.

Parables are, by design, irresistibly allegorical. Indeed, as Brandon Scott (1989) points out, the Hebrew word for parable, *mashal*, comes from the root *m-sh-l*, meaning "to be like." Webster's most generic definition of allegory reads: "the figurative treatment of one subject under the guise of another." The question becomes, then, what are the subjects being treated? This is where the church has too often jumped from trying to understand Jesus' allegory to ourselves *allegorizing the allegory*. Thus every "earthly" subject of Jesus becomes a figure for a "heavenly" topic.

Consider, however, this verse from the poet Daniel Berrigan:

> Under glass, in Met museum
> this day I saw
> a bird of paradise
> outspread
> the grandiose, grotesque
> book of Kells.

This, obviously, is a simile: the book of Kells "is like" a bird of paradise in Dan's apprehension. He is neither being literal nor is he "spiritualizing" the book (both referents are "terrestrial"). The figure of speech illumines the illuminated manuscripts; we are invited to "see" them in a different way.

Jesus was on that kind of mission: to get us to see the world differently: "Do you have eyes, yet fail to see?" (Mk 8:18; see 4:10-12). His pedagogic purpose was twofold:

> 1) to unmask the illusions his audience had about the status quo and their place in it;

> in order to . . .

> 2) open their hearts and minds to what he proposed as an alternative—what he called the "Kingdom of God" (itself a metaphor).

We might call this today "deconstructing" and "reconstructing" consciousness. He thus employs two basic kinds of parables: those that attempted to unmask and critique the way the world *really was* (e.g., "there was a certain rich man ... and a certain beggar...," Lk 16:19f), and those that offered a vision of the way the world *could be* (e.g., "the Kingdom of heaven may be likened unto...," Mt 18:2).

The genius of these stories was that they narrated recognizable scenarios in plain language that any illiterate peasant could understand: farming (Mk 4:1ff) and shepherding (Mt 18:12-14), being in debt (Lk 7:41-43) and doing hard labor (Mt 20:1ff), being excluded from banquets (Lk 14:1ff) and from the houses of the rich (Lk 16:19ff). These vignettes would draw the listener into their familiarity, only to throw a surprise twist in order to challenge popular assumptions about what was proprietary and what was possible: a miraculous harvest (Mk 4:8), an enemy as a friend (Lk 10:33), or unexpected vindication (Lk 18:2ff).

Contrary to our traditional spiritualizing treatment of them, then, parables were "earthy stories with heavy meanings," as William Herzog puts it in his important book *Parables as Subversive Speech: Jesus as Pedagogue of the Oppressed* (1995). To try to illustrate this, let us look at perhaps the best example of the parable as criticism of the way the world is—one that is often misread as if it were a Kingdom parable, with disastrous consequences. I am talking about the notorious parable of the talents (Mt 25:14-30).

This has been for many an unsettling story. It seems to promote ruthless business practices (v. 20), usury (v. 27) and the cynical view that the rich will only get richer while the poor become destitute (v. 29). Moreover, if we assume, as does the traditional reading, that the Master is a figure for God, it is a severe portrait indeed: an absentee lord (v. 15) who cares only about profit maximization (v. 21), this character is hard-hearted (v. 24) and ruthless (v. 30). Despite these concerns, this story still routinely occasions countless homilies (usually on stewardship Sunday!) how we Christians should gainfully employ our "talents" for God—despite the fact that "talent" in the gospel text has nothing to do with our individual gifts and everything to do with economics. Might it be that we have imposed upon the parable our capitalist presumptions about the glories of a system that rewards "venture capital," and thus read the story exactly backwards?

Our first clue lies in the parable that immediately precedes the Talents. A specifically Kingdom figure, the story of the bridesmaids reiterates the traditional gospel exhortation to "stay awake" so as not to be caught unawares by the "moment of truth" (Mt 25:1-13). This story prefigures the drama in the garden of Gethsemane, in which the disciples are urged to remain vigilant for when the time comes to confront injustice. What follows is a story about a very rich master—but there is no indication that this is a *Kingdom* parable (25:14). We have been warned to be alert!

The original audience of this story would not have had to allegorize to make sense of it. Its portrait of a great household—the closest thing in antiquity to the modern corporation—was all too recognizable. The powerful patriarch would often be away on economic or political business. His affairs would be handled by slaves, who in Roman society often rose to prominent positions in the household hierarchy as "stewards" (25:15). But the sums entrusted here border on hyperbole. Scott writes: "A talent was one of the largest values of money in the Hellenistic world. A silver coinage, it weighed between fifty-seven and seventy-four pounds. One talent was equal to 6,000 denarii" (one denarius was an average subsistence wage for a day's labor). If one talent was worth more than fifteen years' wages, we can roughly translate the assets made available for investment at about two and a half million dollars. These are elite financial dealings indeed!

The first two slaves *double* their master's investment (25:16f). Though lauded by modern interpreters, this feat would have elicited disgust from the first century audience. Richard Rohrbaugh (1993) notes that in antiquity the highest legal interest rate was about 12%; anything more than that was considered rapacious. This is the first of many hints that the operations of this household are something less than exemplary.

Bruce Malina (1981) shows how in traditional Mediterranean society, stability was the ideal, not self-advancement. Anyone trying to accumulate inordinate wealth imperiled the equilibrium of society and was thus understood to be dishonorable. Greed was widely believed to characterize the rich, who extorted and defrauded other members of the community through lucrative trading, tax collecting and money lending at interest. In fact, usury was understood in antiquity to be responsible for the destructive cycle of indebtedness and poverty, while profiting from commodity trading was explicitly condemned by no less a sage than Aristotle.

The biblically literate, moreover, would recall the warning against stored surplus in Exodus 16:16-20, the prohibition against usury and profiteering off the poor in Leviticus 25:36f , or Isaiah's condemnation of those who "join house to house and field to field" in their real estate dealings (Is 5:8). Yet Herzog thinks that it is precisely such unscrupulous business dealings that are denounced by this parable.

Large landowners made loans to peasant smallholders based on speculation about future crop production. With high interest rates and vulnerability to lean years and famine, farmers often were unable to make their payments, and faced foreclosure. Once in control of the land, the new owner could continue to make a killing by hiring laborers to farm cash crops. (It is a process of economic exploitation and wealth accumulation that is still all too characteristic of our own global economy.) In the parable, the master's slaves do this highly profitable dirty work well.

We, of course, undaunted by this historical context and blissfully interpreting the parable through capitalist lenses, have nothing but praise for these "good stewards." As Rohrbaugh puts it, "commentators of the 19th and 20th centuries have genuinely reveled in the parable's seeming exhortation to venturous investment and diligent labor." We then turn to castigate the third slave who, cautious and "unproductive," represents an object lesson of entrepreneurial failure (25:18). But if the manner of profiteering portrayed in the story would have been understood by the original audience as rapacious, is it not possible that this non-cooperating third slave might in fact be the *hero* of this parable?

When the master returns to settle accounts we find identical phrasing in his commendations of the first two financiers (25:21,23): "Well done, good and trustworthy slave.... Enter into the joy of your master." We are used to reading this allegorically as connoting entry into heavenly bliss. But at the plain level of the parable it serves not only as a promotion ("I will put you in charge of many things"); it is also a reminder that these handlers are *still slaves*, and that it is the *Master's* joy in which they are participating! We might say that these slaves are more captive than ever to the world controlled by their lord.

Like a good three-part joke, we now come to the punch line: the third slave is about to explain his (in)action (25:24f). That he buried the money in the ground seems strange at first glance. But considering that many in Jesus' audience were farmers, there may be some wry peasant humor here. Those who work the land know that all true wealth comes from God, the source of rain, sunshine, seed and soil. But this silver talent, when "sown," produced no fruit! Here is the clash between two economic worldviews: the traditional agrarian notion of "use-value" and the elite's currency-based system of "exchange-value." Money cannot grow the natural way like seed, only unnaturally, through usury and swindling. Is this symbolic act of "planting" the talent a case of prophetic tricksterism to reveal that money is not fertile?

The third slave now begins to speak truth to power. "I knew you were a harsh man" (the Greek is *skleeros*, a word associated with old Pharaoh's disease of "hard-heartedness"). "You reap where you did not sow, and gather where you did not scatter seed." With these words the third slave becomes what Herzog calls a "whistle-blower," having unmasked the fact that the master's wealth is entirely derived from the toil of others. He profits from the backbreaking labor of those who work the land. Unwilling to participate in this exploitation, this third slave took the money out of circulation where it could no longer be used to dispossess another family farmer.

This courageous dissident embodies the moral of the bridesmaids parable. He has awakened to the rules of the master's world. His repudiation of it is simple and curt: "Here, take back what is yours" (25:25). But he admits that through it all, "I was afraid." For good reason—he is about to meet the prophet's fate.

It is instructive that the Master does not refute this monkey-wrencher's analysis of his world (25:26f). He simply castigates him as "evil and lazy" (the favorite slur of the rich toward those who don't play the game), and wonders rhetorically why the slave didn't at least seek market-rate return. The Master is not interested in "what is my own"—he appreciates only appreciation. He then turns to make an example of the third slave, dispossessing him and giving the spoils to his obedient colleague, in order to illustrate the way the *real* world works: "For to those who have, more will be given ... but for those who have not, even what they have will be taken away" (25:28f).

This parable reads much more coherently as a cautionary tale about the world controlled by great householders (this is even clearer in Luke's version of the story, Lk 19:11ff). As a call to resist the usury system, this parable coheres with the gospel witness to Sabbath economics we have been considering. Indeed, Jesus even may have been spinning a thinly-veiled autobiographical tale here—for he himself will shortly stand before the Powers, speak the truth and take the consequences. On the other hand, to read in this story a divine endorsement of mercenary economics and the inevitable polarization of wealth is to miss the point completely—and to perpetuate both dysfunctional theology and complicit economics in our churches.

To be sure, the consequence of the third slave's non-cooperation is banishment to the "outer darkness where there will be weeping and gnashing of teeth" (25:30). We have presumed this to be "hell," and so perhaps it is—that is, the hell on earth experienced by those rejected by the dominant culture: in the shadows where the light of the royal courts never shine, on the mean streets outside the great households, the dwelling place of the outcast poor like Lazarus (Lk 16:19-21). The story that immediately follows this tragic conclusion—the famous last-judgment parable of the sheep and the goats (Mt 25:31ff)— may illuminate the nature of the dissident slave's exile.

This singular judgment story in the gospels suggests that we meet Christ mysteriously by feeding the hungry, giving drink to the thirsty, welcoming the stranger, clothing the naked, caring for the sick, and visiting the imprisoned (25:25-40). In other words, in places of pain and marginality—the "outer darkness." The whistleblower's punishment kicks him out of the rich man's system, but brings him closer to the True Lord, who dwells with the poor.

We have for too long ignored or trivialized parables as arcane, pedantic or platitudinous, ever hoping to keep aright the world they mean to turn upside down. Our example shows that Jesus used these "folksy" stories to interrogate the most entrenched arrangements of power and privilege, in this case calling for renewed resistance to usurious "business as usual" in Israel, a costly vocation indeed. Only by bringing the parables back down to earth can we encounter their power both to unmask the "real world" in its cruelty and presumption, and to proclaim the radical hope of Sabbath economics.

Chapter Six

"And there was enough..."

Jesus' Wilderness Feeding and the Eucharist as an Economic Ritual

Modern readers usually approach the famous gospel "miracle" story of the loaves and fishes (Luke 9:10-17) with innate suspicion. This is because we are profoundly shaped by the rationalist assumptions of modernity, and so immediately distance ourselves from stories of the "supernatural," in one of two ways. In order to preserve our rationalist assumptions, we might discount the story as primitive legend (bread doesn't just multiply by itself), and if we take it seriously at all, proceed to "rescue" it by a spiritualizing interpretation. In order to preserve the "authority" of the text, on the other hand, we might acknowledge the "miracle" but discount our own capacity to embody such practice (amazing things like that may have somehow happened back then, but not in our world, and not by *my* agency). In either case, we have ruled out the possibility that the central exhortation of this story ("*You* give them something to eat," says Jesus to the disciples, Lk 9:13) might somehow be directed at *us*.

This is reinforced by the way(s) in which the gospel story has *already* been interpreted to us. Often we don't hear the story afresh at all; we hear tapes in our head of old homilies, or our own half-formed theological musings, or church doctrines, or neatly packaged spiritual lessons that lie tucked in the corners of our religious consciousness. Thus we are likely to understand this feeding story as a sort of foreshadowing of the Last Supper, because that is how it tends to be preached from First World pulpits. The story only *appears* to concern realities of hunger or issues of economic distribution (then and now) we assume; what it *really* points toward is the Eucharistic mystery. But the loaves and fishes account is better understood within the context of its "intertextuality" (the referencing and re-narrating of older biblical stories).

Luke's account of the feeding in the wilderness is closely patterned after Mark's (see Mk 6:31-44). As night begins to fall upon a large crowd that has assembled in the wilderness, the disciples urge Jesus to dispatch the people to the neighboring villages to provision themselves (Lk 9:12). To this attempt to solve the problem by relying on the vagaries of "market economics," Jesus responds bluntly: "*You* give them something to eat." While the disciples agonize, incredulous and indignant at the prospect of having to deal with this situation of deprivation, Jesus organizes. Determining the food on hand, he distributes the loaves and fish (9:14-16). A careful reading shows that the only "supernatural" occurrence here is that "all ate and were satisfied" (9:17).

What has often been noted, and what fuels the traditional "eucharistic" reading of this story, is that the formula here ("Take ... bless/give thanks ... break ... give ...") is common to both (Lk 9:17 and 22:19). But narrative common sense must question the assumption that we should read the *earlier* episode in light of the *later* one, when the opposite would be more coherent. In fact, the allusions in the wilderness feeding point back to several earlier sacred stories of the Jewish tradition—which provide a far more reliable lens through which to interpret our text than later Eucharistic theology!

The wilderness setting of Luke's bread story obviously alludes to the story of the manna (Ex 16; see Chapter One). Here, as in Exodus 16, the focus is not upon the "miraculous" but the "gathering" for the purposes of community sufficiency. Less obvious is another old tradition upon which our gospel story is drawing as well: the "food miracles" of the great prophet Elisha (II Kings 4:42-44).

The Elisha story takes place during a time of famine (II Kg 4:38). In the Bible famine is understood not just as an unfortunate natural disaster, but as the result also of human economic systems of greed. Indeed, according to Genesis 47:13ff, the Israelites ended up in Egypt because of Joseph's "management" of famine conditions to benefit Pharaoh's interests.

Like the disastrous flooding in Central America in the late 1990s, these are natural cycles that turn into social disasters because of political and economic conditions of exploitation. Elisha encounters a scene in which local people, driven to desperation by economic breakdown, are forced to return to the ancient ways of hunting and gathering to survive (II Kg 4:39). But these folks no longer have competence in the traditional ways, since sustainable local economic cultures were destroyed by forced integration into the command economy of the empire. Thus these desperate peasants gather gourds that are inedible: "There is death in the pot" (II Kg 4:40). Elisha "heals" the soup pot (4:41), and then turns his attention toward "bread."

The loaves brought to him are made from "new grain" (4:42), inferring that they represent offerings of first fruits appropriate to the early harvest feast of *Shavuot* (see Lev 23:15ff). But while normally these first fruits are offered back to God by the priests, in this crisis Elisha "redirects" them toward those in need. In a line Luke's Jesus will quote, he instructs the provider to "give it to the people to eat" (II Kg 4:42). As in the gospel story, this command is met with incredulity (4:43). But the "Word of the Lord" prevails, transforming the situation of artificial scarcity into a celebration of God's natural abundance: "And they ate and had some left over" (4:44). It is this transformation that Jesus re-enacts in the wilderness.

By following narrative paths back into Torah and the Prophets, we have gained new perspectives on the gospel story of feeding the hungry in hard times. The feeding of the multitudes in the wilderness (a story so important that both Matthew and

Mark narrate it twice) is thus *economic* in character before it is *eucharistic*. The biblical tradition in which Jesus stands asserts that only the divine economy of grace, not the market, can address the problem of deprivation. The practice of Sabbath economics, illustrated by manna in the wilderness and again by Elisha in the face of famine is the tradition that Jesus is "remembering" in a different wilderness in a different time, teaching self-sufficiency through a practice of sharing available resources (what we today might call "cooperative consumption").

The real worlds of both Elisha and Jesus (and indeed of our own global economy) were characterized by widespread hunger and poverty that resulted from a feudal system of land ownership and from an extractive economic system that benefited the urban elite while disenfranchising the rural poor. In such worlds, economic practices of enough-and-then-some for *everyone* were, and are, miraculous indeed.

The first Christians appear to have understood these connections. According to Luke, the inaugural account of the church "breaking bread" animated a thoroughgoing communal redistribution of wealth (Acts 2:42-47). Luke's Pentecost account narrates the "birth" of the church in the power of the Holy Spirit. Yet what *sort* of practice the Spirit empowered at Pentecost, and continues to empower, has been a divisive issue in the life of the church ever since. Today the debate about what it means to be "Spirit-filled" usually focuses on individual charismatic gifts. The roots of Pentecost, however, are agricultural — and thus unavoidably *social* and *economic*. Pentecost was a Jewish observance called the "Feast of Weeks" (*Shavuot*), originally a celebration of the first fruits of the harvest (Ex 23:14-17; Dt 16:9-12). As we saw in Chapter One, the seven weeks time frame of the festival echoed the symbolism of the Jubilee (Lev 23:15=25:8,10).

It is significant, then, that Luke's narrative of Pentecost reasserts the Jubilee implications of the Feast of Weeks. Robert Tannehill notes that the scene commences abruptly with the unusual phrase: "When the day of Pentecost was being fulfilled" (Acts 2:1). This may signal that the original intentions of the Feast are about to be realized in the "first fruits" of the new

49

messianic movement. The narrative opens with "tongues of fire *distributed* among the disciples" (2:3) and ends with them selling their possessions and *"distributing* them to whoever had need" (2:45, the only two appearances of the Greek verb *diamerizoo* in Acts). Peter's talk of the "gift" of the Spirit and the unilateral cancellation of debts in Jesus Christ (v. 38) echoes the Jubilee pronouncement of Jesus' first sermon (Lk 4:18ff). This suggests that Acts 2 may have far more to do with the Jubilee vision of redistributory justice in the cultural and economic spheres than with the individualistic spectacle of glossolalia that preoccupies so much modern Pentecostalism.

It is to be expected that whenever God's Spirit is poured out on people, their traditions and institutions will be disrupted and disturbed. God's intervention is always subversive, because YHWH is not a domesticated deity, baptizing our traditions and institutions, but the One who seeks to liberate us from our enslaved condition, to heal us of our wounds and addictions, and to animate us in the practice of justice and compassion. Thus when the Spirit descends in Acts, it empowers the church to move across established (and enforced!) social and economic boundaries of *gender* (as Peter endorses women prophets, 2:17f), *race* (as the disciples engage in multilingual outreach, 2:9,39) and *class* (as "uneducated, common Galileans" preach to "devout leaders," 2:7).

The Spirit-filled church also speaks hard truth to the unjust authorities, and challenges them to repent (2:14-40). Above all, the "house" is transformed from a hiding place for fugitives (2:2) to a place where Jubilee economics are celebrated at table (2:46), as the "economics of enough" are again embodied in the life of renewed Israel (again, a scene that is so important that Luke narrates it twice in Acts 2:44-47 and 4:32-37). The astonishment of onlookers who encountered *this* sort of church surely lingers in our hearts today as we look at our ecclesial life: "What does this mean" (2:12)?

Nor was Luke's portrait of the Acts church anomalous. Paul, too, understood the breaking of bread to be a social demonstration of solidarity, not just a religious ritual of spiritual salvation. This is most clearly shown by his bitter denunciation of the ways in which the Eucharistic practices of the Corinthian church were mirroring the social stratification of Roman table fellowship, instead of demonstrating equality (II Cor 11:17ff). I will examine this in more detail in the next chapter.

Bread breaking rightly stands at the center of the church's life as an invitation to "remember" — to remember the economy of grace practiced by our ancestors in the faith, and to remember what we ourselves must do to embody an ethic of equality in a world deeply divided between "haves" and "have-nots." Sadly, just as the disciples wanted to send the hungry crowds away to the villages in the wilderness feeding story, so do we today harbor too much faith in the ability of the "market" to meet people's needs.

What would it mean for us to revise our celebration of the Eucharist in light of this biblical tradition of Sabbath economics? Can we re-narrate the wilderness feeding in our own context, whether at a Catholic Worker soup kitchen, or the Jubilee 2000 campaign against Third World debt, or local advocacy for a living wage ordinance? Only such practices can recover the animating power of the liturgical ritual, which together with our sacred stories can interrogate our world and our lives concerning God's dream of equality and dignity for all.

Chapter Seven

"It is a matter of equality."

Paul and Sabbath Economics

What became of Jesus' radical vision of Sabbath economics among his followers? To hear many theologians tell it, the abandonment of these practices came as early as the apostle Paul. It was Paul, they argue, who supplanted the discipleship theology of following Jesus with a mystical Christ-religion, and who promoted a social ethic that conformed to contemporary Greco-Roman standards rather than challenged them. But biblical scholars such as Elsa Tamez (1993), Neil Elliott (1994), and Richard Horsely (1997) in recent works have contended that Paul's writings must be freed from the powerful interpretive biases of modern Protestantism, liberal and evangelical alike, and read instead in their own socio-historical context. They and others are building a case for a Paul who was in fact essentially egalitarian, subversive of imperial religion and politics, and an advocate for the poor.

As I have worked to recover the biblical tradition of Sabbath economics, nothing has been a greater revelation than the new understanding I have of Paul and his message. I believe that Paul understood the "Christ-event" as a "cosmic Jubilee." For him, grace, traditionally understood by Protestants to lie at the heart of his theology, pertains not just to spiritual matters, but invites us to Sabbath redistribution of resources and power as a way of life. Footprints of the Jubilee tradition can be found throughout Paul's pastoral correspondence. The Corinthian epistles provide a wonderful example of how Paul's practice reflected a fundamental concern for social justice, resistance to Roman norms of class stratification, and desire to demonstrate faith commitment by wealth-sharing.

Corinth in Paul's time was characterized by a culture of "new wealth." It had been sacked by the Romans, then rebuilt a century later and repopulated with immigrants, entrepreneurs, military veterans and freed slaves. Located along key trading routes, it was prosperous, ambitious, and competitive—and marked by huge disparities between its "nouveau" elite and its laboring and slave classes.

One of the main themes of Paul's exchanges with the Christians at Corinth springs from his struggle to counter the dominant culture of meritocracy, materialism, and elitism. He continually defends his apostleship against opponents who criticize him for his disinterest in matters of social status, rhetorical style and public performance (II Cor 2:14-5:15). Apparently the Corinthian believers, not unlike many North American Christians today, were impressed with the displays of charismatic power by those who preached a "prosperity theology."

Against such prestige-oriented Christianity Paul pits his own commitment to costly discipleship (II Cor 4:8-11). He contrasts himself with "hucksters of the Word of God" (II Cor 2:17) and those who "pride themselves on position" (II Cor 5:12), defending his apostolic credentials in terms of marginalization rather than status, of suffering rather than self-advancement, and most importantly, of grace rather than merit.

The cornerstone of social stratification in the dominant culture was the Roman system of patronage, and it affected Corinthian Christians at many levels. Bruce Malina and Richard Rohrbaugh (1999) describe the patronage system as "… socially fixed relations of generalized reciprocity between social unequals in which a lower-status person in need (called a client) has his needs met by having recourse for favors to a higher-status, well-situated person (called a patron). By being granted the favor, the client implicitly promises to pay back the patron.... The client relates to the patron as to a superior and more powerful kinsman, while the patron looks after his clients as he does his dependents." Conventions of patronage functioned in economic, social, and political spheres. Ben Witherington (1995) correlates the rise of patronage to two factors. One was the demise of earlier, more democratic institutions in Mediterranean society; as the more hierarchical structures of the empire imposed themselves, patronage increasingly defined all social relations. The other factor was the increasing erosion of the social safety net, which made personal patronage a practical necessity.

Under the patronage ethos it was expected that Paul would support his pastoral ministry in Corinth either by professional religious begging or by positioning himself as an "in-house philosopher" sponsored by a wealthy patron. Paul, however, steadfastly (and in the eyes of many Corinthians, unreasonably) refused to become a client of the rich. Instead, he insisted on supporting himself through a trade (I Cor 9; see I Thess 2:9). This stance offended members of the aristocracy and lowered Paul's prestige in their eyes because he worked with his hands.

Paul recognized patronage as the glue that held all the oppressive relationships of the empire in place. Following the Christ who had been executed by that empire, Paul instead embraced the status of a "slave" (the lowest social class), in order that he might serve all people equally without being beholden to those of high political or economic standing (I Cor 9:18-23). He engaged in this discipline both to model the redistribution of power at a personal level and to subvert the social fabric of the "status quo." This commitment to "downward mobility" was one concrete expression of Paul's commitment to the Jubilee vision of socio-economic equality.

But Paul expected all the Christians in Corinth to reflect new, revolutionary social relationships in their community life. So when in their life together they reproduced (consciously or unconsciously) the divisions of the Hellenistic society around them, he was outraged. We see this reflected in the community's celebration of the Lord's Supper.

Paul approaches the issue of ritual table fellowship by discussing the issue of eating meat sacrificed to idols (I Cor 8-10). This matter was about more than diet and conscience. Most meat available at the market came from temple sacrifices, and only the more affluent in Corinth could afford to eat it. Those scandalized over this practice were the poorer members of the church (probably the majority, see I Cor 2:26). Meanwhile, some aristocratic Christians were interpreting Paul's "gospel of freedom" as license to continue participating in the Roman Temple feasts. These public gatherings were crucial in legitimizing patronage, promotion of the imperial cult, and consolidation of economic-political solidarity among upper classes. Witherington notes that the normal practice at Roman *symposia* was "to rank one's guests in terms of social status, with those of higher status eating with the host in the dining room and others eating elsewhere and getting poorer food." These gatherings were also notorious for turning into drunken orgies.

Worst of all, in Paul's eyes, it seems these same elite and educated Corinthian Christians insisted upon aping such hierarchical class behavior when the church would gather for the Lord's Supper (I Cor 11:17-34). This infuriated the apostle, who denounces such "proprieties" in the strongest possible terms. He calls it "profanation" of the body of Christ, and even speculates whether such abominations might lead to illness and death. Finally, he rhetorically kicks the offenders out of the Christian feast: "If you must eat this way, go home" (I Cor 11:34a).

Paul's objection to such practices, Horsley argues, has to do with his concern for social solidarity. With whom one eats and what one eats form the identity of the body politic. Paul cannot see how Christians can partake of the "one bread" of the poor Christ and the "cup of demons" passed around in the debauched Roman Temple feasts of the rich (I Cor 10:16-21). For Paul, the church was to model an alternative society where there was no patronage, no hierarchy, no rich and poor. This is, then, the second way in which Paul rehabilitated the old tradition of Sabbath economics. Because he believed that in Christ the community of faith is a "new creation" in which "everything old has passed away and everything has become new" (II Cor 5:17), he consequently insisted that the divine economy of grace should displace the habits of Roman meritocracy.

This new way of being is made possible by the fact that "God has reconciled the world to Godself through Christ" (5:18). This famous declaration lies at the heart of Paul's theological argument to the Corinthians. The term "reconciliation" (Greek, *katallagee*) originally referred to an exchange of money in repayment of a debt (we still speak today of "reconciling a bank statement"). Paul's discourse here is more economic than expiatory. Reconciliation entails economic ramifications for community relationships, and Paul's use of the term resonates with Jubilee debt-cancellation. Indeed, such unilateral release is precisely the meaning of God's decision "not to count their trespasses against them" (5:19).

But in order to participate in this new social order we must accept God's reconciliation of accounts—the "cosmic Jubilee." Thus Paul calls believers to embrace the "ministry of reconciliation" (5:18), to become "ambassadors" for Christ (5:20a). The title ambassador designated official envoys of Caesar. In appropriating it, Paul directly challenges the public order. Caesar's ultimatum through his ambassadors may be, "Submit to imperial rule!" but God's appeal through the emissaries of Christ is, "Be reconciled to God" (5:20b)!

If we wish to "cooperate" with God's project, warns Paul, we must be prepared to practice this divine economy of grace in our own social life. Otherwise the cosmic Jubilee is "in vain" (6:1)—one of Paul's more sobering (and hence widely ignored) theological assertions. He then quotes Isaiah 49:8, a hymn to the liberation of Israel from captivity: "*Now* is that day!" (II Cor 6:2) Paul's rhetorical strategy of existential urgency echoes Luke's portrait of Jesus' inaugural sermon. Jesus reads Isaiah's vision of the Jubilee, then comments, "*Today* this scripture has been fulfilled" (Lk 4:21). Following Jesus, Paul worked to recontextualize in the contemporary community the Jubilee teachings of Torah.

Most significant for our discussion is the collection Paul orchestrated among his churches on behalf of economically disadvantaged Christians in Jerusalem, a project so important that he mentions it in almost every epistle (see I Cor 16:1-4; Rom 15:25-32; Gal 2:10). In II Corinthians 8-9, we encounter his most elaborate discussion of his rationale, and it is here that the apostle directly appeals to the scriptural tradition of Sabbath economics.

Paul cannot *demand* that the Corinthian church participate in the collection, because this would be contrary to the order of grace (II Cor 8:8). So he employs instead a variety of rhetorical strategies to persuade, some of which are almost amusing. First Paul points to the generosity of other communities, hoping either to shame the Corinthians or to inspire them to friendly competition (8:1-7). Then he points to Christ's example of "class defection" (8:9). Finally he issues a strong "advisory" (8:10-12) before moving on to explain the principle behind the practice he is trying to promote (8:13ff).

Paul is concerned that the Corinthians will interpret his appeal to share wealth according to the expectations and conventions of patronage. But the obligatory and dependent nature of the patronage relationship was precisely what Paul wished to avoid. He was asking for Christian justice and solidarity, not charity or patronage (see II Cor 9:5-7). For this reason, he refers to the project ten times in II Corinthians 8-9 as the work of "grace" (Gk *charis*). Paul, the great apostle of "grace alone," here makes it clear that it is not just a theological concept. It *must* include practices of economic sharing. Paul opens and closes his appeal to the Corinthians by reminding them that this financial partnership only mirrors the grace of God (8:1; 9:14), and whatever largess they muster will only dimly reflect God's "indescribable gift" (9:8,15).

Young and Ford (1987) point out that Paul's vocabulary of "abundance" throughout II Corinthians (see 1:5; 7:4; 11:23) contradicts this notion of "limited good" that characterizes the dominant economic discourse. "Subsistence with stability was the main aim of economic activity for most people, and the right to subsistence was closely bound to one's family and its inherited place in society. It was an economy in which equilibrium, not growth, was the ideal. This was supported by a network of relationships based on informal reciprocity, enforced by the powerful appeal to honor and shame." In contrast, Paul understood God as the "central resource" who injects unlimited good into this economy. "It is all for your sake, so that grace may extend to more and more people" (II Cor 4:15). Because of this, the circulation of goods and services within the church should be determined by God's overflowing grace and gift rather than the economics of scarcity and patronage (II Cor 9:6-14).

In a carefully crafted doublet, the apostle articulates the "golden rule" of Jubilee: "Not that others should be relieved and you afflicted; rather, it is a matter of equality. So in this time your surplus should help their lack so that their surplus might help your lack—in order that there may be equality" (II Cor 8:13f). The term "equality," so important to modernity, appears in the New Testament only here and in Colossians 4:1. ("Masters, treat your slaves justly and as equals"—a phrase meant to subvert, not legitimate, the hierarchical structure of Roman slavery.) Then, in his only scriptural warrant for the collection project, Paul directly evokes the Jubilee tradition: "The one who had much did not have too much, and the one who had little did not have too little" (II Cor 8:15). This is, of course, the central "instruction" of the wilderness manna story (Ex 16:18), the foundation text of Sabbath economics.

It is germane that the recipient of Paul's collection, the "mother church" in Jerusalem, was already itself practicing the economic sharing Paul was exhorting (at least according to Luke's Acts account that we examined in the last chapter; see Acts 4:34f). Paul is thus urging his Hellenistic congregations to embrace what the Palestinian church had apparently established as Christian "orthopraxy." Along this vein, we might note that in Paul's version of the famous "Jerusalem council compromise" reported in Acts 15, the one matter everyone agreed on despite their cultural differences was that "the poor should be remembered" (Gal 2:10).

By understanding Christ's life and death as a "Jubilee-event" Paul invites us onto a path of grace which seeks constantly to redistribute power, prestige and resources "as a matter of equality." Not only does Paul set a personal example by refusing Corinthian patronage and insisting that the church there do the same, he also invites these Gentile Christians to practice international economic solidarity with a minority that was widely despised in the Hellenistic world: Palestinian Jews.

Today, the crushing burden of indebtedness and profound inequality imprisons more and more people in First and Third Worlds alike. If our North American churches are to advocate for redistributive justice for the poor, we, like the first century Corinthians, will have to cease mirroring the dominant culture of the global capitalism, with its empty promises of upward mobility and trickle-down justice. We must turn toward the biblical vision of Sabbath economics, which is central not only to the Hebrew Bible and the Jesus-tradition, but to Paul's pastoral strategy as well. The apostle insisted that only disciplines of redistribution can overturn our calcified traditions and structures of charity, class entitlement and meritocracy. For Christ "took on" the debt system in order that "we might become the justice of God" (II Cor 5:21).

Conclusion

Reflections on Addiction, Recovery and Sabbath Economics Today

The great obstacle is simply this: the
conviction that we cannot change
because we are dependent upon what is
wrong. But that is the addict's excuse,
and we know that it will not do.

Wendell Berry

The biblical vision of Sabbath economics continues to haunt our history. Having just turned the millennial corner, Sabbath economics is again firing the imaginations of faith-based activists who are looking for new models of justice at a time when political paradigms are shifting. But those of us who would insist that the Bible's ancient socio-economic and spiritual disciplines remain relevant in our context have hard work to do. We must diligently and creatively explore what contemporary, concrete analogies to Jubilee practices of old might be today. It will take real political imagination to discern how ideas of Sabbath debt-release spawned in radically different historical and socio-economic periods might be recontextualized for our own situation. In order to nurture commitment and creativity we would do well to promote the following in our communities of faith:

- "Jubilee literacy" in our biblical and theological reflections on all aspects of faith and life;
- an applied spirituality of forgiveness and reparation in both interpersonal and social spheres;
- practical economic disciplines for individuals, households and congregations around questions of consumption, finances, and work;
- participation in political movements addressing issues of local, national and international social-economic policy.

Unfortunately, the relationship that we affluent North Americans have to things economic is not rational, and no simple set of rational exhortations to change will suffice. Our relationship is in fact characterized by compulsion (we can't imagine doing things differently) and powerlessness (what can one person do?). Wendell Berry is right—these are the hallmarks of "the addict's excuse." Feminist community organizer Barbara Brandt (1995) has examined addictions to work, consumption and money in her excellent book, *Whole Life Economics*. If the problem we are facing is indeed one of addiction, it will be helpful in conclusion to reflect briefly on the task in front of us in terms of "recovery." This means we must develop communal programs of accountability, covenant and discipline.

A fruitful beginning place for Christians might be to reimagine the three great "evangelical disciplines" articulated in the old monastic Rule of St. Benedict (490-543 C.E.): poverty, chastity and obedience. The early monks understood three key things about the dominant culture of their time:

1) It was built upon the concentration of wealth and exploitation. If their communities were to repent they must become as self-sufficient as possible.
2) The root of wealth-concentration was private property. If they wanted to resist the "temptations of the world" they must renounce exclusive ownership.

3) The exploitation of human labor was the root of all alienation (Marx later rediscovered this). If their communities were to restore human dignity they must practice manual (that is, unalienated) labor.

For the first monastic communities the vow of "poverty" actually intended to inspire a social model that would *eradicate* poverty. This analysis would seem to still obtain today.

Contemporary North Americans "… spend $5 billion a year on special diets to lower their calorie consumption, while the world's poorest 400 million people are so undernourished they are likely to suffer stunted growth, mental retardation, or death," writes Alan Durning (1990). The affluent clearly need disciplines other than compulsive diets and obsessive gym workouts, which only mask our addiction to consumerism! The vow of "poverty" today might represent the equivalent of steps one through three in the Twelve-Step tradition. To recognize our public addiction to economic privilege and power means keeping the dysfunctional and deadly disparity of wealth always in view, and daily deciding to "turn over" our economic lives to the alternative reality of the divine economy of grace.

Three household disciplines of "economic sobriety" come to mind. The "simple living" movement has been well documented (see Neal, 1977; Finnerty, 1977). As a spiritual discipline, so-called "downward mobility" is necessary but not sufficient, as it too easily can remain a private (and for many, a privileged) strategy. Experiments in communal common purses, collectivist living and co-housing arrangements, while difficult to sustain under capitalism, nevertheless encourage the recovery of traditional practices of extended family and hospitality that have atrophied in modern urban culture.

Groups such as the Ministry of Money and Harvest Time, that grew out of the Church of the Saviour in Washington, D.C., have developed processes specifically for affluent people, including exposure tours to poor countries and suggestions for personal economic partnerships. Other groups, such as Self-Help Credit Union of North Carolina, are trying to help individuals and churches invest responsibly, particularly given the need for capital in poor neighborhoods (see Brill, et al, 1999; Meeker-Lowry, 1995; Kinsley, 1997). Three of the best sources for finding resources on all these issues and initiatives are: Alternatives for Simple Living (www.simpleliving.org); the Center for a New American Dream in Washington D.C. (www.newdream.org); and *Yes! A Journal of Positive Futures* (www.futurenet.org).

A second discipline, that of building local organizations that promote economic responsibility concerning land, labor and capital, takes us more into the public struggle. Cooperative work strikes at the heart of alienated and alienating wage-labor, as do some the emerging "green" and socially-responsible business practices. Local living wage ordinances should be supported, and churches need to rediscover their historic solidarity with trade unions. Land trusts and agricultural or environmental conservancies represent an alternative to private ownership, and community money systems and the burgeoning Community Supported Agriculture movement address the challenge of "re-communitizing" the marketplace. The pioneering work of Chuck Matthai's Equity Trust organization is modeling new property relationships that express a "social revaluing" of land, labor and capital in order to equitably balance both public and private interests.

A third and even better discipline of recovery is making *ourselves* available to the poor. People of privilege should socially relocate to live and work in proximity to disenfranchised people not primarily in order to "help," as in the old missionary model, but in order to view the world *from that space*. We thus avoid liberal abstractions about poverty and begin to build relationships with poor people. I have found community among the very folk against whom I had been "insulated" by my suburban, middle class upbringing. The longer we are rooted in such neighborhoods, the more the issues so familiar to the poor become our own. Our work then moves from "aid" to "alliance," from sympathy to solidarity.

Such disciplines expressing a "vow of poverty" no more make us poor than do those of an institutionalized monk today.

But they do create the conditions for engagement with bigger structural issues, because our awareness of public addiction is heightened in direct proportion to our *actual* discontinuity with it. Lifestyle changes are not a political *solution* to anything, but can represent a political *question* to everything. As Herbert Marcuse (1969) put it: "No matter how great the distance between the middle-class revolt in the metropoles and the life-and-death struggle of the wretched of the earth—common to them is the depth of the refusal."

Behind traditional vows of "chastity" lay the early monks' profound appreciation of the fundamental connection between flesh and spirit. Economic practices, like sexuality, are not inherently evil; they are intrinsic to our humanity. But our appetites—economic and sexual—are exploited mercilessly by the highly sophisticated techniques of seduction in capitalist culture. Recovery thus also involves a kind of "consumer celibacy" toward commodity fetishism (the visceral belief that we are made happy or better by the stuff we own or use). Rather than yielding to the promises and obfuscation of marketers, we reassert responsibility for what we buy, investigating what conditions the product was made under, who profits from it, what its environmental impact is, and so on (see the excellent work on youth, identity and consumerism available at www.adbusters.org and in books by Lasn, 1999, and Kilbourne, 1999). This represents steps four through seven of the Twelve Step program: the ongoing struggle to remove the addictive behavior from our lives.

In this case, chastity is not a private vow, but a discipline of collective accountability. We middle class people are hostages to deeply ingrained assumptions about private ownership, freedom and control. This extends not only to material things but also to use of time, space, vocational options and above all, decision-making. Nothing challenges our socialization into the fictive autonomy of the consumer more viscerally than accountability for how we earn and how we spend, because we *actually* (not hypothetically) have to give up private control. More accurately, however, we are *taking back* control from the expectations of the market. Such disciplines are the only way to discover how deeply we are possessed by our possessions, and are the most effective means of facilitating recovery.

Finally, the vow of "obedience" was understood by the monks to represent single-minded attentiveness to the will of God. Here it means living in fidelity to the cosmology of Grace and the practices of Sabbath economics. This requires both a defensive strategy of non-cooperation with the social and economic imperatives of the public addiction, and an offensive strategy of engagement with the political Powers. War tax resistance, for example, is a household spiritual discipline of refusing to cooperate with the political economy of militarism, as well as an act of citizenship responsibility I believe to be more meaningful than voting.

Because public addiction is legal, the vow of obedience may often lead to civil *disobedience*. The current anti-globalization movement that became widely visible with the historic 1999 "disturbances" at the World Trade Organization meetings in Seattle represents a real surge in popular and international civic resistance to the worst trends of neo-liberal capitalism. This broad coalition of grassroots advocacy groups is probably the most dynamic and populist social movement for change in the world today, fueled mainly by youth and crossing many issue and constituency boundaries. Christians should be participating!

Other forms of political action include promoting economic literacy at the grassroots and organizing consumer education and actions, from boycotts to shareholder protests. A Catholic priest, for example, was acquitted by a Chicago jury in 1990 after a campaign of defacing neighborhood billboards advertising alcohol and tobacco products that ravage the lives of so many in his urban, working class, Black and Latino parish. In South Central Los Angeles, churches and community groups organized to prohibit the rebuilding of liquor stores after the 1992 Uprising, and ended up fighting a white political establishment "under the influence" of the powerful alcohol lobby.

Rabbi Arthur Waskow (1995), who has written extensively on *shabat*, recommends that people of faith focus on three major areas of public policy development: venture capital recycling, mandatory sabbaticals for the research and development sector, and neighborhood empowerment and celebration. Other strategies include participation in labor organizing, zoning battles, class-action lawsuits, and of course political lobbying campaigns, such as the significant efforts of the Jubilee debt-relief movement (www.j2000usa.org). There are many consumer, public interest and corporate watchdog organizations that would welcome the support of churches, such as Corporate Watch (www.corpwatch.org) and the Alliance for Democracy (www.igc.org/alliance).

None of these forms of engagement in personal and political transformation, however, can be sustained or deepened without the central spiritual discipline of Sabbath-keeping. Increasingly both Christians and Jews are re-visioning what Sabbath renewal might look like in light of our political situation of crisis. Many are returning to the healing (and subversive) character of regular rhythms of rest and "non-productivity" for both individuals (see Lerner, 2000; Muller, 1999; Harris, 1996) and for society as a whole (i.e. the recent "Free Time/Free People" project, Shalomctr@aol.com).

The tasks before us are as imperative as they are daunting. In the face of the unaccountable markets and "capital-idolatry" of the runaway global economy, we must work to restore real and non-exploitative relationships between producers, distributors, consumers and the earth itself. The integrity and fate of our planet, our society and our faith tradition are all at stake.

Can we embrace the spiritual disciplines of recovery in a society in the grip of a fatal addiction? God's grace *is* sufficient. "As those who would cooperate with God," pleaded the apostle Paul, "we urge you: Do not receive God's gift in vain.... I tell you, *now* is the time of God's favor; *now* is the day of salvation" (II Cor 6:1f).

References Cited

Berry, Wendell. What are People For? North Point Press, 1990.

Brandt, Barbara. Whole Life Economics: Revaluing Daily Life. New Society, 1995.

Brill, Hal, J. Brill and C. Feigenbaum. Investing with Your Values: Making Money and Making a Difference. Bloomberg Press, 1999.

Collins, Church and F. Veskel. Economic Apartheid in America: A Primer on Economic Inequality and Insecurity. New Press, 2000.

Durning, Alan. How Much is Enough? The Consumer Society and the Fate of the Earth. W.W. Norton & Co., 1992.

Elliott, Neil. Liberating Paul: The Justice of God and the Politics of the Apostle. Orbis, 1994.

Finnerty, Adam Daniel. No More Plastic Jesus: Global Justice and Christian Lifestyle. E. P. Dutton, 1977.

Harris, Maria. Proclaim Jubilee! Westminster/John Knox Press, 1996.

Haughey, John. Virtue and Affluence: The Challenge of Wealth. Sheed & Ward, 1997.

Herzog, William. Parables as Subversive Speech: Jesus as Pedagogue of the Oppressed. Westminster/John Knox, 1994.

Horsely, Richard, ed. Paul and Empire: Religion and Power in Roman Imperial Society. Trinity, 1997.

Kilbourne Jean. Deadly Persuasion: Why Women and Girls Must Fight the Addictive Power of Advertising. Free Press, 1999.

Kinsler, Ross and Gloria. The Biblical Jubilee and the Struggle for Life. Orbis, 1999.

Kinsley, Michael. The Economic Renewal Guide: A Collaborative Process for Sustainable Community Development. Rocky Mountain Institute. 1997.

Lasn, Kalle. Culture Jam: The Uncooling of America. Eagle Brook, 1999.

Lerner, Michael. Spirit Matters: Global Healing and the Wisdom of the Soul. Walsch Books/Hampton Roads Publishing, 2000.

Lowery, Richard. Sabbath and Jubilee. Chalice Press, 2000.

Malina, Bruce. The New Testament World: Insights from Cultural Anthropology. John Knox Press, 1981.

Malina, Bruce and Richard Rohrbaugh. A Social-Science Commentary on the Synoptic Gospels. 1999.

Marcuse, Herbert. An Essay on Liberation. Beacon Press, 1969.

Meeker-Lowry, Susan. Invested in the Common Good. New Society Publishers. 1995.

Meeks, Douglas. God the Economist: The Doctrine of God and Political Economy. Fortress Press, 1989.

Muller, Wayne. Sabbath: Restoring the Sacred Rhythm of Rest. Bantam, 1999.

Neal, Mary. A Socio-theology of Letting Go: The Role of a First World Church Facing Third World Peoples. Paulist Press, 1977.

Prior, Michael. Jesus the Liberator: Nazareth Liberation Theology. Sheffield Press, 1995.

Ringe, Sharon. Jesus, Liberation, and the Biblical Jubilee. Fortress Press, 1985.

Rohrbaugh, Richard. "A Peasant Reading of the Parable of the Talents/ Pounds," Biblical Theology Bulletin, 23:1, Spring 1993, pp 32ff.

Scott, Brandon. Hear Then the Parable. Fortress Press, 1989.

Tamez, Elsa. The Amnesty of Grace: Justification by Faith from a Latin American Perspective. Abingdon, 1993.

Waskow, Arthur. Down-to-Earth Judaism: Food, Money, Roots and Branches: Sex, and the Rest of Life. William Morrow and Co, 1995.

Witherington, Ben. Conflict and Community in Corinth. Eerdmans/ Pater Noster Press, 1995.

Yoder, John Howard. The Politics of Jesus. Eerdmans, 1972.

Young, Frances and David Ford. Meaning and Truth in Second Corinthians. Eerdmans, 1987.

Other Resources of Related Interest

"The Ad and the Ego." Video on the subtexts of advertising available from California Newsreel (www.newsreel.org)

"Affluenza" and "Escape from Affluenza." Public Broadcasting System specials available on video (www.pbs.org/kcts/affluenza/home.html)

Barber, Benjamin. Jihad vs. McWorld. Random House, 1995.

Berry, Wendell. Home Economics. Northpoint Press, 1987.

Brecher, Jeremy and Tim Costello. Global Village or Global Pillage: Economic Reconstruction From the Bottom Up. South End Press, 1994.

Brown, Lester. State of the World 2000. W.W. Norton, 2000.

Brown, Robert McAfee. Kairos: Three Prophetic Challenges to the Church. Eerdmans,1990.

Canadian Ecumenical Jubilee Initiative. Jubilee, Wealth and the Market. CEJI, 1999.

Cassidy, Richard. Jesus, Politics and Society: A Study of Luke's Gospel. Orbis, 1979.

Cobb, John B. Sustaining the Common Good: A Christian Perspective of the Global Economy. Pilgrim Press, 1994.

Daley, Herman and John Cobb. For the Common Good: Redirecting the Economy Toward Community, the Environment, and a Sustainable Future. Beacon Press, 1989.

Diamond, Jared. Guns, Germs and Steel: The Fates of Human Societies. Norton, 1997.

Duchrow, Ulrich. Alternatives to Global Capitalism: Drawn from Biblical History, Designed for Political Action. International Books/Kairos Europa, 1995.

Frank, Thomas. One Market Under God: Extreme Capitalism, Market Populism, and the End of Economic Democracy. Doubleday, 2000.

Hartmann, Thom. The Last Hours of Ancient Sunlight: Waking Up to Personal and Global Transformation. Three Rivers Press, 1998.

Jameson, Fredric. Postmodernism, or The Cultural Logic of Late Capitalism. Duke University Press, 1991.

Kavanaugh, John. Following Christ in a Consumer Society. Orbis Books, 1989.

King, Paul, Kent Maynard and David Woodyard. Risking Liberation: Middle Class Powerlessness and Social Heroism. John Knox Press, 1988.

Marcuse, Herbert. One Dimensional Man: Studies in the Ideology of Advanced Industrial Society. Beacon Press, 1964.

May, Gerald. Addiction and Grace. Harper & Row, 1988.

Meadows, Donella, Dennis Meadows, and Jorgen Randers. Beyond the Limits. Post Hills, VT: Chelsea Green, 1992.

Myers, Ched. Who Will Roll Away the Stone? Discipleship Queries for First World Christians. Orbis, 1994.

Schaef, Anne Wilson. When Society Becomes an Addict. Harper & Row, 1987.

Schumaker, E.F. Small is Beautiful: Economics as if People Mattered. Harper, 1973.

Sklar, Holly. Chaos or Community? Seeking Solutions, Not Scapegoats for Bad Economics. South End Press, 1995.

Slater, Philip. Wealth Addiction. E. P. Dutton, 1983.

Ucko, Hans, ed. The Jubilee Challenge: Utopia or Possibility? Jewish and Christian Insights. Geneva: WCC Publications, 1997.

Vallely, Paul. Bad Samaritans: First World Ethics and Third World Debt. Orbis, 1990.

Wachtel, Paul. The Poverty of Affluence: A Psychological Portrait of the American Way of Life. New Society Publishers, 1989.

Williams, William Appleman. Empire as a Way of Life. Oxford University Press, 1980.

Other Publications by Ched Myers

Liberating Biblical Study: Scholarship, Art and Action in Honor of the Center and Library for the Bible and Social Action (Wipf & Stock, 2011), edited with Laurel Dykstra. *Paper, 278 pp.*

Ambassadors of Reconciliation (Orbis, 2009), with Elaine Enns.
Vol. I: New Testament Reflections on Restorative Justice and Peacemaking. Four N.T. studies on restorative justice and peacemaking. *Paper, 192 pp.*
Vol. II: Diverse Christian Practices of Restorative Justice and Peacemaking. Three analytic models and nine profiles of contemporary Christian practitioners of restorative justice and peacemaking. *Paper, 193 pp.*

Binding the Strong Man: A Political Reading of Mark's Story of Jesus: 20th Anniversary Edition (Orbis, 2008/1988). This full-length commentary on Mark's Gospel, using a socio-literary method, is considered a classic. *Paper, 550 pp, new Preface & Intro.*

Who Will Roll Away the Stone? Discipleship Queries for First World Christians (Orbis, 1994). This sequel to *Binding the Strong Man* is a comprehensive articulation of a North American theology of liberation, justice & peace. *Paper, 495 pp.*

Say to This Mountain: Mark's Story of Discipleship (Orbis, 1996), With M. Dennis, J. Nangle, C. Moe-Lobeda and S. Taylor. A popular version of *Binding the Strong Man*, combined with reflections on the contemporary relevance of the text to today's context. Ideal for study groups. *Paper, 240 pp.*

All books, as well as more than 100 of Ched's published articles can be downloaded and/or purchased online at

www.ChedMyers.org